The Fisherman
of
Halicarnassus

Roger Williams

bb

Bristol Book Publishing
London

Other books by Roger Willliams

Fiction
Aftermath, A-Train, Burning Barcelona,
Father Thames, High Times at the Hotel Bristol,
Lunch with Elizabeth David

Non-fiction
The Royal Albert Hall: A Victorian Masterpiece for the 21st Century,
The Most Amazing Places to Visit in London,
London Top 10, Eyewitness Barcelona and Provence,
Berlitz Dubrovnik and Tenerife
& many other travel books and guides

All fiction titles are available as ebooks

The Fisherman of Halicarnassus
The man who made Bodrum famous

Cevat Şakir Kabaağaçlı
"Halikarnas Balıkçısı"

1890–1973

This edition published in the UK by Bristol Book Publishing
www.bristolbook.co.uk

The Fisherman of Halicarnassus
ISBN: 978-0-9567416-6-0

Printed and bound by CPI Group (UK) Ltd, Croydon, CR0 4YY

CONTENTS

Spelling and pronunciation

Turkish spellings have been used in most cases. Cevat Şakir Kabaağaçlı is pronounced Shee-vat Sha-keer Kaba-atch-ler. Ş is sometimes anglicised as *sh*, ğ is hardly pronounced at all and an ı without a dot is *uh*.

Constantinople and Smyrna did not change their names to Istanbul and Izmir until the 1930s, and they are both used, according to the period being written about. The dots on their capital 'i's are not used, as the names are common in English.

Halicarnassus and Herodotus are more correctly Halikarnassos and Herodotos, but their Latinised names have for so long been used in English that they have become anglicised, as has Homer. Similarly, 'c's are in common usage in English for Caria and Lycia rather than ancient Greek 'k's.

ACKNOWLEDGEMENTS

A number of people have been helpful in the preparation of this book. Sema Sagat, founding Curator of the excellent Bodrum Maritime Museum, gave valuable assistance. George Bass, Professor Emeritus at Texas A&M University and founder of the world-wide Institute of Nautical Archaeology, kindly checked the relevant text. I am grateful to Serpil Oppermann, Professor of English at Hacettepe University, Ankara, for translations from her paper on *The Fisherman's Narratives of the White Sea (the Mediterranean)*. Marc Dubin, a Samos resident and colleague in the travel-writing business, fact checked and added some choice snippets. Pam Barrett's support, encouragement and critical proof-reader's eye were as essential as ever.

My Blue Voyages began with Loes Douze, the eternally sunny SCIC Sailing operator whose hard-working captains and crews have taken me to many of the inspiring places mentioned in this book.

ANATOLIA

AEGEAN SEA

MEDITERRANEAN SEA

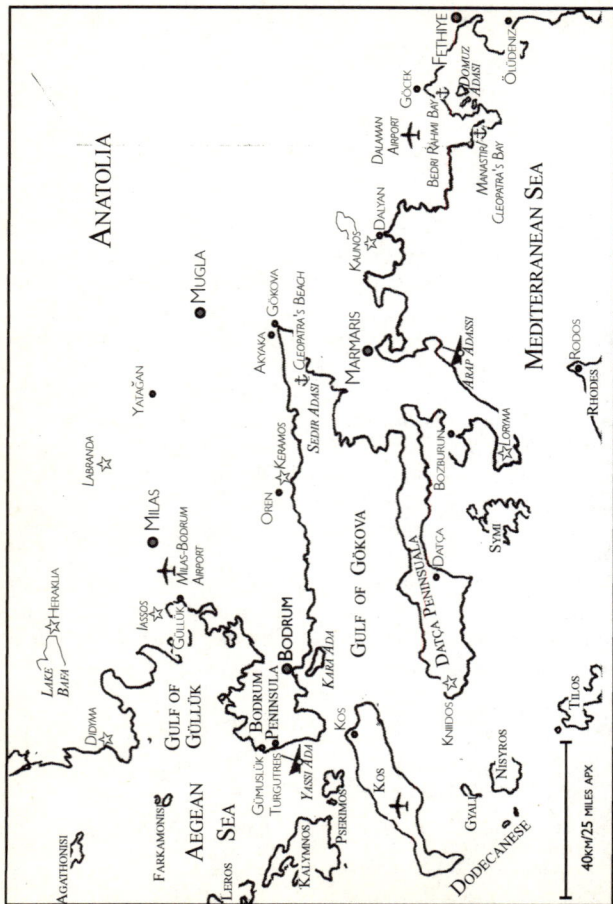

Blue Voyage waters

MUĞLA

YATAĞAN

LABRANDA

MILAS

IASSOS

HERACLIA

LAKE BAFA

DIDYMA

GULF OF GÜLLÜK

GÜLLÜK

MILAS-BODRUM AIRPORT

BODRUM PENINSULA

BODRUM

GÜMÜŞLÜK

TURGUTREIS

YASSI ADA

KARA ADA

KOS

PSERIMOS

KALYMNOS

LEROS

AGATHONISI

FARKAMONISI

GULF OF GÖKOVA

ÖREN

KERAMOS

SEDIR ADASI

AKYAKA

GÖKOVA

CLEOPATRA'S BEACH

MARMARIS

ARAP ADASSI

BOZBURUN

LORIMA

DATÇA PENINSULA

DATÇA

KNIDOS

SYMI

RODOS

RHODES

TILOS

NISYROS

GYALI

DODECANESE

DALYAN

KAUNOS

DALAMAN AIRPORT

GÖCEK

DOMUZ ADASI

FETHIYE

ÖLÜDENIZ

BEDRI RAHMI BAY

MANASTIR BAY

CLEOPATRA'S BAY

40km/25 MILES APX

8

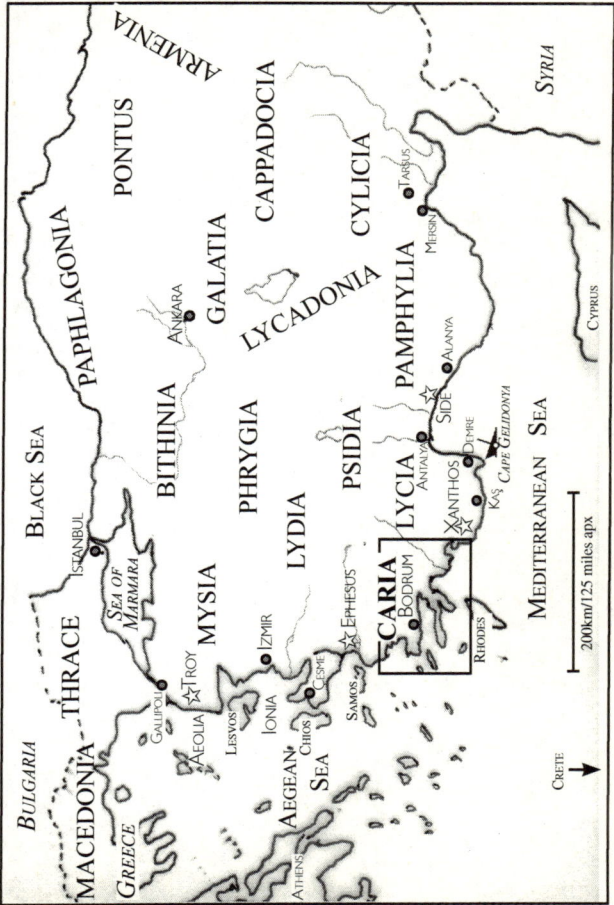

Regions of Asia Minor in antiquity

1. MERHABA!

"If you come to the top of this hill, you will see Bodrum. Don't think that you will leave the same person as when you arrived. To all those who came before you, it happened that way: they lost their hearts in Bodrum."

This quotation is the first thing visitors see on the main road into Bodrum. It is written large on a sign of welcome erected by the town council with a photograph of the smiling, weather-battered face of its author. He is Cevat Şakir Kabaağaçlı, known as 'Halikarnas Balıkçısı', the Fisherman of Halicarnassus, and his name will crop up again and again on a visit to the town he is credited for turning into Turkey's most famous resort.

His words in praise of Bodrum and its blue waters find their way on to every scrap of travel literature, on walls of hotels, and even on paper tablecloths set out for breakfasts. His bust is outside the castle and it sits in a memorial garden in Cevat Şakir Caddesi, the main street, where the Bodrum Maritime Museum has a corner dedicated to his life.

The Fisherman lost his heart here when he arrived in 1925 as a prisoner, sentenced to internal exile by a tribunal of the new Turkish Republic for something he had written. He found and fell in love with what was then an impoverished village of fishermen and sponge divers, of narrow lanes trudged by camels and donkeys where people went to bed when the sun went down, and he stayed to see it become a fashionable and lively summer resort that today likes to party till dawn.

Cevat Şakir was an Oxford-educated writer and artist from the upper stratum of Ottoman society. What caused him to take up his pen-name was life in the community that he encountered here, a life far removed from the one into which he had been so fortunate to have been born. Here the people, like their ancestors, "could look on things unperturbed by cant and prejudice – just the naked eye of man gazing on nature".

His stories gained him a wide national readership, but he became involved in the community, too, improving fishing techniques and planting trees in public spaces. He has even been described as 'the first ecologist'. In the 1950s and 1960s literary and artistic friends came to see him, and to join him in the simple summer adventures he had been enjoying for more than two decades, sailing with minimal provisions and equipment around the Gulf of Gökova and along the Carian and Lycian coasts. Soon these 'Blue Voyages' or 'Blue Cruises' began to appear in holiday brochures that put Bodrum on the map and brought the first adventurous travellers from abroad, so that in time many of the fishermen who had inspired the Fisherman were able to hang up their hooks, stow their nets and find employment in the more lucrative and less perilous tourist trade.

This coast is the meeting point of the Aegean and Mediterranean seas. Into their blue waters tumble the last folds of the majestic Taurus mountains that rise over the Mediterranean littoral of Lycia before drifting down to the shore in myriad bays and islands. On the west coast, mountain ranges run parallel with the shore and there are few entry points into the interior. It is these mountains that helped to keep the coast cut off for centuries, leaving Anatolia's exceptionally rich plant life to bury countless layers of Classical civilisations.

Here is to be found the densest concentration of Greco-Roman remains in the world. The province of Muğla, in which Bodrum resides, has no fewer than fifty-seven sites, more than any other in Turkey. There is such a proliferation of rock tombs, temples, arenas, theatres, necropolises and city foundations that even in the 21st century many acres remain in desperate need of archaeological investigation.

Halicarnassus, the ancient name for Bodrum that predates the Greeks, was an important city, the capital of Caria, and famous for the enormous tomb of its ruler, Mausolos, which became one of the Seven Wonders of the World. Ephesus, which possessed another Wonder, lies to the north; the island of Rhodes, to the east, had a third.

By seeing Anatolia from the coast, as the travellers of antiquity had done, the Fisherman and his friends identified many sites that archaeologists would subsequently come to explore. These discoveries led Cevat Şakir to believe that Anatolia was the wellspring not just of Classical Greek culture, but of all Western civilisation. He eventually settled to the north of Bodrum in Izmir (Greek Smyrna), Aegean Turkey's main city, where he became the country's first professional tourist guide. It was in this city, he liked to recall, that his hero Homer was most probably born. His epic poems that chronicled the siege of nearby Troy in the *Iliad* and Captain-King Odysseus's subsequent adventurous homeward voyage in the *Odyssey*, were texts that Şakir returned to again and again.

As the Fisherman of Halicarnassus, he wrote extensively on the legacy of Asia Minor, which the West calls Anatolia, the Greek for 'east'. In Turkish it is Anadolu. The Fisherman's thoughts were synthesised through voyages with his friends

13

who joined him in Bodrum on his Blue Voyages, and between them they developed a philosophy that combined classical literature with nature, mixed in with a belief in the common 'folk' to arrive at 'Blue Anatolian Humanism'. Though they were not involved in politics, their beliefs brought them into conflict with the authorities and they all at some point found themselves in jail.

Even before the extraordinary events of his life unfolded, both happiness and tragedy seemed to be etched in Cevat Şakir's features, as his young sister, Fahrelnisssa, recalled in her diary after one of his visits from Oxford: "*He had the oddest face. The upper part seemed to be crying, while the lower part looked as though it were laughing. It was as if one had cut out the top part of a tragedy mask and glued it to the bottom of a comedy mask.*"

He aged well. In 1977, four years after Cevat Şakir's death, the journalist Ian Crawford wrote a piece in *New Scientist* recalling an encounter a few years earlier in Bodrum, where he found the Fisherman "*lying on his boat in the bay with the tiller between his feet…a handsome old man, who spoke seven or eight languages with commanding fluency, wit and erudition. He talked of Homer as if he had just left him in a pub down the road, of how the hexameter had been born of a dance rhythm formed with the fingers of one hand, and of Pegasus on a petrol station sign blushing from head to toe at being used in an advertisement.*"

Mentions of the Fisherman of Halicarnassus in an English publication are rare. Though he is still highly regarded in Turkey, where his books – five novels, eleven books of short stories and eleven books of essays – sell around 2,000 copies a year (not including pirated copies), it is hard to find any of his work in translation. In 1993, twenty years after his death, a fictionalised film of *Mavi Sürgün* (*Blue Exile*), Cevat Şakir's own story of his banishment to Bodrum, was made by the Turkish director Erden Kıral.

This book is not a biography or a literary critique. It is a guide book for modern Blue Voyagers, a small volume to take on board to dip in and out of, to fill in a few key facts about Turkey and about just a few of almost fifty civilisations that have flourished here, and to give a flavour of Cevat Bey and the waters he sailed. In the process it attempts to answer the question any tourist arriving in Bodrum may well ask. Who exactly was this Homeric figure called the Fisherman of Halicarnassus? Why was he so anxious to welcome visitors to Bodrum? And what can he tell us about Turkey and Blue Voyages today?

2. HERODOTUS

The story of the Aegean begins with Homer and the ten-year siege of Troy, started because Paris, the son of King Priam of Troy, ran off with Helen, the wife of Sparta's King Menalaos, who then set out with his neighbour and brother-in-law King Agamemnon of Mycenae to seek revenge. At the time there was no such place as Greece, and no Hellenes. All around the Aegean and Mediterranean were kings and tyrants who formed allegiances whenever it was expedient. Islands like Odysseus's Ithaca, near Corfu, had independent kings. It seemed a mythical time, and the fact that the tales are packed with gods and goddesses made readers believe that the whole Troy business was a fanciful tale, and that even Homer himself might have been an invention. But in the 19th century, with much fanfare, the German archaeologist Heinrich Schliemann who had been digging around the Troad plain, 300km north of Izmir, reached the treasures of the ancient city.

It was only in the late 20th century that most scholars agreed that Homer probably lived around 850BC. This confirmed what they had already been told by Herodotus of Halicarnassus, who wrote that Homer had lived around four hundred years before his own time. Moreover, Herodotus thought the whole Troy episode – a war between allied armies from a land by his time called 'Hellas' against the 'Asiatic' Trojans, a side that included Carians as well as many 'Greeks' – unnecessary, and he blamed the Greeks for starting the conflict. *"Abducting young women is not, indeed, a lawful act,"* he wrote in *The Histories, "but it is stupid after the fact to make a fuss about avenging it. The only sensible thing is to take no notice, for it is obvious that no young woman allows herself to be abducted if she does not wish to be."*

Homer's *Iliad* and *Odyssey* are the epic tales for the Blue Voyager. But if there is one book to read, either on holiday when tucked in the plump cushions on the aft deck of a gulet, or when dreaming away dark winter days, it is *The Histories*, in which Herodotus of Halicarnassus describes the world as he found it on his travels from the Black Sea to the Nile. The author's nine books make a single paperback of nearly 700 pages, a volume that is as easy to dip into as the cool waters of an evening bay. They give a 5th-century BC view of a world surrounded by a great river called Ocean, riven with cults and superstitions, and full of peoples of extraordinary diversity, tempers and predilections.

In his quest for the truth, Herodotus has become known as the father of history, but he was also the father of journalism, sceptical of rumour and gossip and determined to find out the facts for himself. For the Fisherman of Halicarnassus, as for the modern traveller, *The Histories* was a starting point, a deep dive into the Anatolian shore in which the myriad surrounding archaeological remains stand mute. If Cevat Şakir Kabaağaçlı's exile to Bodrum was the making of him, exile *from* Halicarnassus was the making of Herodotus. The two men stand like bookends, back to back. While both shared an endless curiosity about people and their environment, one's voyage of discovery was local, internal, the other's was broad and far ranging. Towards the end of his life, Cevat Şakir wrote *A History of the Civilisation of Western Asia*, which, like *The Histories*, looked at the whole world between the Black and Red seas. He had hoped it would be translated

17

into English. Both men came from well-to-do families. The noble household into which Herodotus was born around 485BC was well connected. His father, Lyxes, was Carian, and his mother, Dryo, like the Fisherman's mother, Cretan, and he was also a close relation, perhaps a nephew, of Panyassis, writer of epic poems. Panyassis is not the first name that comes to mind when thinking of Greek literary figures, but he was important, and his influence on Herodotus must have been crucial. Among his screeds of epic poetry is Ionia, a 7,000-line poem that deals with the Ionian settlement of Asia Minor, so perhaps it is unsurprising that much of what we know of the history of the region comes from Herodotus, who must have heard lines such as these many times.

The first Greeks migrants were Dorians, inhabitants of parts of the Peloponnese and islands to the south, including Crete. They began arriving on the coast around the 10th century BC, and in Bodrum initially settled a trading post on Zephysia, or Zephyros, then an island, where the crusader castle now stands. They gave their name to the Dorian Peninsula on the opposite side of the Gulf of Gökova, called Datça today. Ionians from Attica arrived later, settling on the Aegean seaboard around Izmir, and by Herodotus's time Ionian was the common dialect of the Greeks of Halicarnassus. The native Carians had their own language. Without comment, Herodotus gives the prevailing theories of the origin of the Carians. According to the Cretans, he says, they were islanders known as Leleges, who had invented crests for helmets, and devices and hand grips for shields, all three ideas adopted by the Greeks. But the Carians themselves claimed to be mainlanders and their shrine to Zeus at Labranda near Milas had been established long before the Greeks arrived. We may never know. Carian inscriptions, dating no later than the 4th century BC, have yet to be deciphered. Greeks and Carians by and large mixed well, in trading as well as in marriage. Queen Artemesia I, who was on the throne at the time of Herodotus's birth, had a Carian father and Cretan mother. The Carian community lived opposite Zephyros on the safe heights of Salmakis Hill. They mixed freely in the *agora*, the market place by the seafront between the two settlements – Bodrum's harbour has long been a place where many languages and dialects can be heard.

The Carian town had developed around a spring, which, like the best ancient watering holes, had a mythical tale to tell. It had been inhabited by a nymph called Salmakis, after whom the hill, now topped with windmills, is named. She had fallen in love with a beautiful young boy, Hermaphroditos, and she prayed that they might be united in love. Her prayers were answered: the gods bonded them physically into a figure that was both male and female. As a result, the waters of the Salmakis spring had a reputation for causing any man drinking from them to become effeminate. It is easy to imagine the curious young Herodotus heading for the sanctuary of Hermaphroditos to take a sip just to see if the rumour were true. His masculinity still intact, he may at that moment have begun wondering what else in the world wasn't quite as it was said to be, and needed to be confronted to be confirmed.

A noble family such as Herodotus's might have lived in a hillside villa overlooking the port, with roses, quince and figs in the garden, and evenings of gossip about the comings and goings on the islands and coast, of news of cargoes and festivals, of omens, alliances, uprisings.

They would talk about politics, too. Like other Anatolian regions, Caria was not powerful enough to exist alone. Cities combined in federations, seeking alliances that suited them best. In the Hexapolis of the original Doric settlements, for example, Halicarnassus formed an alliance with Knidos, the nearby island of Kos and three cities on the island of Rhodes, until it was expelled after one of its athletes behaved badly at the annual games. Increasingly, power was polarised between west and east, Greek and Persian, though Greeks on the Aegean coast often took the Persian side. The naval battle of Salamis, which effectively ended the second Persian invasion of Greece, occurred during Herodotus's childhood, and the story of the conflict forms much of his *Histories*. He was about five years old when Artemesia I, Queen of Halicarnassus, had commanded the Carian triremes in the Persian fleet of more than a thousand vessels against the victorious Greeks. The wars secured Athens' hegemony over the Aegean, so Caria became in league with the Greeks, though satraps and tyrants still made their own laws.

For all his examination of the world about him, Herodotus does not tell us much about his city or himself. We don't know why his uncle fell out with Artemesia's grandson, Lygdamis II, or what crimes led to the poet's execution in 454BC, when Herodotus would have been around thirty. It may have been a plot to overthrow the tyrant, and although there is no telling how it might have involved Herodotus, he had been exiled with his family to the island of Samos at some point in his younger life, and from there his travels began. There was no looking back.

Though he wrote little about Halicarnassus, he does say that the Ionians *"had the good fortune to establish their settlements on a region that enjoys a better climate than any other we know of"*. Carians and Ionians, he learned, were the first foreigners to settle in Egypt, where they were employed as mercenaries. After the great festival of Isis at Busiris, a crowd of "tens of thousands" beat their breasts in honour of the god, but

Carians went further, cutting their foreheads with knives "to show they were foreigners".

Not only did he collect stories on his travels, but he recited them too, which accounts for their lively, conversational style. He became famous for his tales, and always drummed up a large audience at festivals and symposia. In Athens, he would have known Sophocles and other leading lights of the day, and he recited his 'histories' at the Olympiads – not all of them, as they would have taken more than two days and nights to read aloud.

To his audience, he was simply reporting on the marvels of man and nature that he had encountered and, just as importantly, what the people he had met had to tell him about their histories and customs, for the Greek word *historia* had no particular connotation with the past, it just meant 'inquiry' or "investigation". They were no more 'histories' than the stories that Bodrum sponge divers told to Cevat Şakir.

3. THE MAUSOLEUM OF HALICARNASSUS

Just about everyone has heard of the Seven Wonders of the World but not many people can name them. The Great Pyramid of Giza is easiest to recall because it is still standing, and perhaps the Colossus of Rhodes, because it seems so bizarre that a statue could straddle the entrance to a harbour. But the tomb of a little-known ruler, Mausolus of Halicarnassus, doesn't always immediately spring to mind. All that is left of the mausoleum that gave its name to any monumental tomb is a few bits of stone and slices of columns scattered about an excavated pit. But if the Fisherman of Halicarnassus could have had his way, there would be more to see than this.

Before he had ever set foot in Bodrum, and not realising that the town would one day be the heart and soul of his life, Cevat Şakir Kabaağaçli had seen Mausolos and his wife, Artemisia II, in London. Since 1882 the giant marble statues of the rulers, along with sculptures of a horse, friezes and other fragments from the tomb, had been displayed in the specially built Mausoleum Room next to the Elgin Room in the British Museum.

A little more than two decades after the treasures had gone on display, Cevat Şakir arrived at Oxford to study modern history. His family home was on Büyükada, largest of the Princes Islands and a ferry ride from Istanbul. Since the age of ten he had been a boarder at Robert College, the prestigious American school in the city, founded by Christopher Robert, a New York philanthropist and Huguenot descendant with a missionary zeal. Now part of Boğaziçi University, it was the first American school to be founded outside the United States.

Cevat seems to have been a rebel from the start, and his willful, independent streak soon rubbed up against the authorities. His writing – or lack of it – was a continual source of conflict. He became sick of praying and bored with all the religious references, he later said, and he was punished for refusing to write about what he had learned in church on Sundays. He was also punished for writing about the mischief his dormitory mates got up to, which caused him to refuse to write anything at all. What he enjoyed was the library, which he found was "full of life", so when his behaviour caused him to become the lone student among 700 to be banned from using its shelves, his friends brought him books to read beneath the blankets in bed, aided by the newly invented battery-operated torch.

In 1907, reluctant to leave the family home to go to Oxford, he picked "the easiest subject" and spent the next three to four years "trying to forget what I had learned there". But he did spend time in libraries, both at his college and at London University, and he learned to speak "marvellous" Oxford English, according to his niece, Şirin Devrim. "*Each word, crisp and clear, exploded in the air*," she wrote in *A Turkish Tapestry: The Shakirs of Istanbul* (the title transliterates from Şakirs, as does her name on the book, which is given as Shirin).

His father had also studied at Oxford. They came from a family of scholars who could trace their ancestry to a village called Elmalı near Antalya from around the time of the arrival of the Seljuk Turks in the 11th century, corresponding to another historical moment: the Norman conquest of Britain.

Later they settled some 300km north in Kabaağaç from which they took their name, and then in neighbouring Afyon, where they still had an estate and an opium farm. Cevat's father, Şakir Pasha, was an historian and soldier, and had been in trouble for supporting the reforming Young Turks, as had his older brother, Cevat Pasha, a historian, diplomat and for three years Grand Vizier, the equivalent of prime minister, before being sent into exile by Sultan Abdülhamit II. In spite of these upsets, with wide literary and cultural interests, the family was as at home in Berlin or Damascus as it was in Constantinople.

Stepping out in white spats, dressed for what he called "the icy hell of Oxford" in a double-breasted Chesterfield coat with velvet collar, Cevat had much more in common with his elite fellow English students than with Turkish fishermen.

In London, a visit to the British Museum would have brought back memories of his young childhood in Athens, where his father had served a stint as ambassador and where he and his older step-brother had played among the ruins of the Acropolis. Now he saw, and admired, the marbles from the Parthenon, removed and brought here a century earlier by Lord Elgin, British Ambassador to the Sublime Porte. To reach the Elgin Room, he would have had to pass through the Mausoleum Room, and here he would have stopped short. The fact that he knew nothing of Halicarnassus or King Mausolos surprised him. Though William Michael Ramsey, a leading authority on Classical Anatolia, was then teaching at Oxford, it was commonly held that Western civilisation had its roots in the Classical Greece of Athens, Macedonia and Sparta. He checked the guide book, and saw the place marked on a map on the wall. What other treasures like these could be lurking in his homeland?

Ten feet tall, the marble figures of Mausolos and Artemisia are every inch a king and queen. Mausolos's round face and full lips are more Asian than European. His beard and moustache are trim and a great lock of wavy hair hangs down to his shoulders. He could be a rock star today. Of course, it was just the fashion of the time. Rich men wore their hair long, and paid an extra tax for the privilege. Artemisia was also of her time, her hair in three rows of braiding, though the years have been unkind to her face, which looks eaten away. She is barefoot, while her husband's sandals could have been bought in the town any time in the past 2,000 years. Both wear similar *chitons*, the fabrics' folds tumbling about their shoulders and thighs, with a second swathe of cloth, a *chimation*, scooped up over what is left of their arms.

Looking at Mausolos and Artemisia, Cevat Şakir saw two figures that proved what he came firmly to believe, that there was no such thing as Western culture or Eastern culture: there was only culture. Nothing existed alone or free from influence. Everything was dependent on history and environment, on time and place. Culture was as fluid and illusive as light, and could not be claimed by any single nation. But he also wondered if there were some things that history books, so devoted to ancient Greece and Rome, had overlooked.

The son of the founder of the Hectomid dynasty, Mausolos was a satrap of the Persians. Enlarging the Carian territory, he moved the capital from inland Mylasa (Milas) fifty kilometres south to the port of Halicarnassus where he created a city and a navy to be reckoned with. During the twenty-four years of his reign he built a palace on Zephyros where Greeks had settled, and encircled his city with a seven-kilometre defensive wall. It encompassed a temple and theatre and a number of other large buildings in the Greek style, for though Mausolos had allied the Carians to Persia, his own taste was for the Hellenic.

Greek artists were called upon to design his colossal memorial: a vision in the sky forever looking down on his people who would remember him each time they glanced heavenwards. It was completed after his death in 352BC by Artemisia II, who was his sister as well as his wife – Carian nobility liked to keep the gene pool small. In all probability the marble images in the British Museum stood side by side in a four-horse chariot fifty metres from the ground. Nobody knows exactly what the great tomb looked like, though a number of people have had a stab at reimagining it, based on ancient writers such as Pliny the Elder, who reported on it nearly four hundred years after it was built. In his *Natural History*, he wrote:

"On the south and north sides it extends for 63 feet, but it is shorter on the front side, the total length of the circuit being 440 feet; the tomb is 25 cubits high and is surrounded by 36 columns. Skopas did the carving on the east side, Bryaxis on the north, Timotheos on the south, and Leochares on the west, but before they had completed the work the Queen died. They did not stop working, however, until it was complete. For above the peristyle there is a pyramid, which is equal in height to the lower part and tapers toward the top in pyramidal fashion with 24 steps; at the top there is a marble quadriga, which Pytheus made. With this added, the total height of the building comes to 140 feet."

This bold amalgam of East and West, of Egyptian, Persian and Greek, was surrounded by a colonnade of Ionic pillars, with sculptures of lions and gods. Two sets of friezes depicted battles: Centaurs versus Lapiths, and Amazons versus Hellenes. Pliny's description of the Mausoleum was, incidentally, used by Nicholas Hawksmoor to design the tower on the spire of St George's Bloomsbury near the British Museum, which he topped with a figure of George I in a Roman toga. The student Cevat Şakir may have noticed this, too.

The monument stood for around 1,500 years, until 1304 when an earthquake struck and the whole lot came tumbling down, shattering Mausolos's statue into dozens of pieces. The resulting heap of marble provided a supply of building material, which was appreciated by the locals as well as the Crusader Knights when they were reinforcing their medieval castle. Ready-cut solid blocks could be heft into place, and the marble could be burned to make lime for mortar. After the Crusaders had done their worst, opening up the tomb and exposing its remaining treasures to plunder, the site was left to the elements. Plants grew over it, worms turned the soil around it, buildings rose, and nothing was left to be seen.

In the subsequent centuries the Ottoman Empire expanded to stretch from Russia to the Red Sea, from Algeria to Azerbaijan, yet beyond the routes of travelling ambasssadors and merchants little was known of its Anatolian core.

At the start of the 19th century, the empire started to crumble, and as it did so, windows on the Classical world began to open. First, the Napoleonic invasion of Egypt revealed the secrets of ancient Egypt. Then came Elgin's marbles, the stunning sculpted frieze from the Parthenon in Athens, which so startled Western collectors and scholars. Without access to the Ottoman lands, they had up until this moment imagined that Rome was the source of the finest Classical art. Now they had to concede that Rome had borrowed, copied and bought from the Greeks. In no time Greeks, who had been without their own country for longer than the Jews, joined the century's revolutionary nationalist movements, spurred on by Lord Byron. Independence brought the fledgling country, region by region, island by island, into the open, and soon light would start to shine eastwards on to Anatolia, as its crucial importance in the Classical world began to dawn on the West.

Charles Thomas Newton made the first and by far the boldest expedition into Anatolia. After working for the antiquities department of the British Museum, he secured the post of vice consul on the island of Lesbos within sight of the Anatolian shore, with a mission from the museum to scout out antiquities. It was then that he came upon the friezes decorating Bodrum castle, and he was determined to discover whatever else remained of the Mausoleum.

Ever since Admiral Nelson had destroyed the French fleet in Egypt, the Ottomans had been an ally of the British, who were now helping them in their fight against the Russians in Crimea, and soon after his return to London in 1856, Newton was able to obtain from the Ottoman court a *ferman*, a legal note for permission to dig around Bodrum in search of the lost Wonder of the ancient world. The British government gave its backing for a thirty-month expedition that would include the ruins of Knidos on the south side of the Gulf of Gökova. The Royal Navy was enlisted, and the Royal Engineers provided a unit of sappers to do the excavating, with two corporals detailed to take photographs. Even taking Heinrich Schliemann's excavations of Troy and Mycenae into account, Newton's archaeological campaign has been described as the most extensive in the 19th century.

It took nearly two months to locate the site of the Mausoleum. The castle and theatre areas revealed nothing. But using information supplied by Pliny and other ancient writers, and on the reckoning of Robert Murdoch Smith, commander of the Royal Engineers, Newton purchased a plot of land in the centre of town where sappers began to attack with pickaxe and spade. This was the right spot, and as more and more of the ruins were uncovered, so Newton bought more land.

Among the first items to be revealed was the head and neck of a colossal horse, with bronze bridle and bit, and part of a wheel, all from the quadriga that had topped the monument. Near it was the statue of the woman presumed to be Artemisia, and seventy-seven marble fragments that would be reassembled by the museum into the statue of Mausolos himself.

At the end of the first year, the expedition moved on to Knidos at the tip of the Datça peninsula, due south of Bodrum on the opposite side of the gulf. Here, during a chilly winter, the expedition procured the six-ton lion, made from a single block of marble, which Cevat Şakir would have seen in the British Museum's Mausoleum Room (it is now a highlight of the Great Court). Three British naval ships were needed to take the plunder of Bodrum and Knidos away. To add to the booty, the marble blocks of the entire north wall of the Mausoleum were demolished and put on board. They would be ideal for building a harbour wall that the British navy was constructing in Malta.

So what Cevat Şakir saw when he arrived in Bodrum some sixty years later was the mess that Newton's expedition had left behind: a large rectangle dug out of the centre of town. He knew at once where the best finds had gone. During his time in Bodrum and later, when he moved to Izmir to find work and for his children's education, the Fisherman of Halicarnassus trawled through the past, researching and writing books and articles on the art and architecture of Anatolia. With no modern guide books to aid them, the Fisherman and his friends on the early Blue Voyages had to rely on Classical Greek geographers Pausanias from Lydia and Strabo, who was born by the Black Sea, as well as the Roman writers Vitruvius and Pliny the Elder, to lead them towards the ancient sites. It meant that they approached the sites as the ancients had done, from the sea, the eternal highway on which they depended. In this way the early Blue Voyages opened up the whole area to archaeological discovery.

For many people, as with the Fisherman, the British Museum is a starting point for an acquaintance with this region. Apart from the Mausoleum and the lion of Knidos, finds from the surrounding area come from Xanthos, Bargylia, Priene and Labranda. In the Ephesus Room are fragments from another Wonder of the Ancient World, the Temple of Artemis. Ephesus lies on the Aegean between Bodrum and Izmir, where Cevat Şakir found work as a tourist guide. With his great knowledge of the classics, and the ability to quote large chunks in a variety of languages and accents, he would inspire anybody visiting ruins from Troy and Pergamon to Sardis and Side. Among those he showed around Ephesus was Georges Pompidou, and afterwards the French president declared: "I have finally met Homer."

Cevat Şakir's only works published in English were officially sponsored booklets about antiquity in western Anatolia. *Asia Minor*, a seventy-two page publication mainly about Ephesus, was produced by Izmir Interpreter-Guides and Tourism Association in 1971. *The Sixth Continent*, published by the Ministry of Foreign Affairs in 1991, is a curiosity. The title refers to the lands around the Mediterranean and there are 128 pages of text. An Art Nouveau-style of colour illustration by the author was used for the cover, as well as eight of his drawings, complemented by photographs from Turkey's best-known photographer, Ara Güler. The fulsome eight-page introduction, written eighteen years after the Fisherman's death, is unsigned, the illustrations are not captioned, and the text dwells largely on the ancient history of Anatolia, galloping forward from the Roman occupation for just six pages until it abruptly ends with the conquest of Constantinople by Mehmet II. Whether this is an unfinished manuscript is not clear, but what is clear is the author's diminishing interest as the centuries turn towards 1,600 years of Byzantine and Ottoman history.

It became Cevat Şakir's mission to promote Turkey's

wealth of Classical ruins. He also wanted to educate local people into understanding the value of the heaps of old columns and chunks of masonry that had for so long been lying around them, and so treat them with due respect. To his eternal regret, however, he never saw Newton's spoils returned to Bodrum.

More than anything, he would have liked to see the sculptures of the most famous rulers of his adopted home town restored to their original place. In his campaign to have them returned, he even wrote to the Queen, asking for them back, saying that they were not meant to live under the grey skies of England. The letter was passed to the British Museum (though they have no record of it), where a curator apparently wrote to thank him for bringing the matter to their attention. As a result, he said, they had painted the ceiling of the Mausoleum Room blue.

4. PRISON

In 1914, on the family farm in Aryon, Cevat Şakir shot his father dead. The circumstances surrounding this event have never been made clear, and he never talked about it. There are many reasons to believe there were tensions between the two. The spendthrift young dandy was interested in poetry and had ambitions to be an artist, but Mehmet Şakir Pasha, historian and diplomat, had wanted him to follow the family occupations of soldier and statesman, and there had been arguments and quarrels.

Those were uneasy times for the Ottoman Empire, which had long been described as "the sick man of Europe". The First Balkan War had wiped out most of its territory in Europe, the Sultan was ineffective and a coup had installed the Union and Progress Party led by Enver Pasha, who was about to take the empire into the First World War on the side of Germany. It was a time to take sides. An argument in the farmhouse could have been about politics, loyalties, money, lifestyle, or some family grievance. Or it could have been a crime of passion.

During his Oxford days, Cevat Şakir became "an eccentric and a fop", according to his niece, Şirin Devrim. Arguments with his father about his extravagant lifestyle were exacerbated when Cevat quit Oxford for Rome to enrol in the Academy of Fine Arts. There he fell in love and married an artist's model, Aniesi. It was on his return with his pregnant wife that the fatal encounter with his father occurred. Had his father disapproved of his bride? Or had the 59-year-old brother of the Grand Vizier attempted to seduce his son's wife? And had he succeeded? That was the suggestion put forward in the 1993 film *Blue Exile* by the director Erden Kıral based on Cevat Şakir's autobiography *Mavi Sürgün* (Cevat was played by Can Togay, Aniesi by Tatiana Papamoskou).

The key facts of the case were the subject of lasting speculation, and his family would never speak of it, but it was certainly a terrific scandal. Cevat Şakir was tried in Constantinople and sentenced to fourteen years imprisonment. Jail for such a flamboyant aristocrat must have been a mighty shock to the system. From out of the limelight, he was plunged into the dark, and however many strings his friends and family were willing or able to pull, it must have seemed to him that his life had stalled, that he would enter this Stygian tunnel as one of the *jeunesse dorée* and emerge the other side in rusty middle age. Much good would his accomplishments in art and languages do him now. He would need to rely on his wits to survive.

Prison kept Cevat Şakir out of the First World War, in which the Aegean Sea played a crucial part, especially after the Allies launched the Gallipoli Campaign in an attempt to capture the Dardanelles, the narrow straits that led to Istanbul and the Black Sea. Allied ships blockaded Smyrna and Salonica (then still part of the Ottoman Empire), and the islands of the Aegean became the scene of cat-and-mouse chases by minelayers, submarines, warships, troop carriers and supply vessels. A secret forward U-boat base was established by Germany in the Gulf of Gökova and Bodrum came under naval bombardment.

The first shelling was in May 1915, a few weeks after the Gallipoli Campaign began. Alfred van der Zee, German

Consul in Smyrna, wrote to the German Ambassador in Constantinople:

"According to advice received, English & French cruisers have successively destroyed all the floating craft of every kind and nature existing at Bodrum, Güllük, Dikili & Foça; this, it is said, in view to hinder any assistance to the German submarines. Before starting the destruction of the craft at Bodrum, a boat that was sent from the French warship Dupleix to reconnoitre having approached within the firing power of the town has been destroyed by the land forces. Six of the sailors of its crew that were captured alive were sent to Smyrna as prisoners. In order to revenge themselves the French shelled the town & a number of buildings have suffered considerably."

The shells toppled the minaret of the mosque in Bodrum castle, and prisoners being held in its cells were transferred elsewhere for their own safety.

In July, short of fuel and needing repairs, a 90-foot long German coastal Unterseeboot, UB14, was towed into the Gulf by an Austrian destroyer. The submarine had just sunk the Italian armoured cruiser *Amalfi* with a loss of sixty-seven lives. Lt-Commander Heino von Heimburg and the crew of fourteen had to wait for a maintenance team to be sent to Bodrum from Constantinople, arriving by train and camel. After being repaired, the U-boat headed back into the Aegean. It had not gone far when it sighted first a hospital ship, which it let pass, then, just off the coast of Kandilousa, an islet south of Kos, it sank the unescorted troop ship *RMS Royal Edward* with a single torpedo and the loss of around a thousand British lives.

The troops had been heading for Gallipoli (Gelibolu). An Anglo-French naval bombardment had failed to take the heights, and this had been followed by a beach landing of 30,000 troops, with contingents from India, Australia and

New Zealand. The campaign had been devised by Winston Churchill, First Lord of the Admiralty, who had expected little resistance. Its failure cost him his job. The hand-to-hand fighting was horrendous, and a Turkish army commander, Mustafa Kemal, who would later be dubbed Atatürk – 'father of the Turks' – called on the 57th Regiment: "I do not order you to fight, I order you to die." The entire regiment was wiped out and there has never been a 57th regiment in the Turkish army ever since. Anzac beach, scene of slaughter of New Zealand and Australian troops, is remembered in both countries on April 25, Anzac Day (Arıburnu in Turkish). Today, visitors to the Gallipoli Peninsula Historical National Park can read Atatürk's words of reconciliation, etched on a marble memorial:

"Those heroes that shed their blood and lost their lives... You are now lying in the soil of a friendly country. Therefore rest in peace. There is no difference between the Johnnies and the Mehmets to us where they lie side by side now here in this country of ours... you, the mothers, who sent their sons from faraway countries wipe away your tears; your sons are now lying in our bosom and are in peace. After having lost their lives on this land, they have become our sons as well."

The high drama of war passed Cevat Şakir by. From his incarceration in Constantinople, he can only have known about the progress of Gallipoli and other major confrontations second-hand, through rumour and gossip. His wife was back in enemy Italy with their daughter, and though his mother visited him, she did so in secret, not wanting his siblings or anyone else in the family to know.

After serving seven years he was released, possibly because he had contracted tuberculosis, though this was usually a fatal disease in those days. There was also a general amnesty of all political prisoners in July 1921. He emerged not into the Ottoman Empire he had known all his life, but into a country at war. Constantinople was divided into three sectors that had been occupied by the British, French and Italians for the past three years, and would continue to be occupied by them for two years to come. In fact it was uncertain whether the Allied powers would ever relinquish Constantinople at all. From a newly claimed capital in Ankara, Mustafa Kemal, hero of Gallipoli, was now waging a desperate three-year War of Independence against an invading army of Greeks in a struggle for Turkey's very existence.

Cevat Şakir's marriage did not survive his imprisonment, and after his release into the occupied city, he went to live with a blind uncle in Üsküdar on Istanbul's Asian shore, where he married the old man's daughter, his first cousin Hamdiye, and soon they had a son. From here he began to rebuild his career as a writer, cartoonist and illustrator. His contribution to the War of Independence was with his pen. Cartoons in the satirical magazine *Güleryüz* (*Smiling Face*) included MP Ali Kemal, a supporter of the Allies and opposed to the national resistance, in a chamber pot.

Şakir also designed the first colour magazine cover to be published in Turkey. "I had been painting from dawn till dusk even before I learned how to write," he once said.

His time in jail had given his material more of a purpose, an edge. One of his articles, titled 'How do prisoners sentenced to be hanged go knowingly to what awaits them', appeared in the pictorial weekly *Resimli Hafta* on April 13, 1925. The story was one he had heard in prison, of army deserters executed without trial. Those in power saw the piece as an incitement for desertion. He and the periodical's owner, Zekeriya Sertel, were accused of "alienating the public from military service" and brought before one of the

Independence Tribunals that had been set up by the new Republic in Ankara. The prosecutor demanded the death penalty for them both.

Just four years after completing his sentence for the killing of his father, Cevat Şakir was once more given a term of imprisonment. Thanks, it has been suggested, to the intercession of a relation, who was a judge, both he and Sertel received just three years, to be served in exile. The designated prison for Şakir was a fortress on the southwest corner of Anatolia in a town called Bodrum. But from his visits to the British Museum in London, Cevat Şakir knew it better as Halicarnassus. It may have been the back of beyond, but it might hold some interest, if ever he could find a way of leaving his cell to visit it.

Around the turn of the century Bodrum's Castle of St Peter the Liberator had been a useful prison for the enemies of the paranoid Abdülhamit II. With the empire under threat, and unrest at home, he saw subversion everywhere. It was a time of intrigue and of informers, like Pascali (Ben Kingsley in the film of Barry Unsworth's book *Pascali's Island*), who had continued to send reports to the Sultan even though many of them were never read.

In *Siren's Feast*, American Nancy Mehagian describes the fate of her grandfather, Samuel, who was arrested in the predominantly Armenian town of Hadjin in eastern Anatolia in 1911 and sent, with nineteen other prisoners, to Bodrum castle. They walked more than a thousand kilometres, shackled together with iron collars. "*When the men faltered they were lashed with whips or jabbed with bayonets,*" she wrote. "*My grandfather languished in that prison dungeon, chained neck and feet to other men. There were no windows and the cell had dirt floors, where dead bodies had been buried six inches below.*"

Eventually, after the intervention of American missionaries

37

in Hadjin, the group was released from Bodrum castle, and Samuel fled to the United States.

There are many skeletons in the castle's story, some the victims of its builders, the Order of the Knights of St John. A precursor of Britain's St John Ambulance Service, the Order was divided among the linguistic groups of the crusaders, each 'tongue' taking responsibility for a particular part of the defences. Answerable only to the Pope, Germans, Italians, French, Spanish and English came together in their cause, even though sometimes the nations were at war with each other.

To begin with, the Order saw its duty primarily as hospitallers, but after Saladin's capture of the Kingdom of Jerusalem put paid to crusading in 1271, they continued to harass Muslim shipping and protect Christian fleets. Driven from the Holy Land, they had briefly settled in Cyprus before moving to Rhodes. From here, they set up stepping stones on the islands that formed a link around the Gulf of Gökova on this vital corner of Anatolia, maintaining fortresses on Leros, Kalymnos, Kos and Nisyros.

As the Byzantine Empire tottered, the knights gained a toehold on the mainland at Smyrna, and when this was overrun by Tamerlane, they joined forces with the Ottoman Mehmed Çelebi to drive the Moghul scion of Ghenghis Khan from the city. This was a time of an interregnum among Turkish rulers. The Seljuk Turks, who preceded the Ottomans, set up a system of *beyliks*, or provinces, in Anatolia. The Beylik of Menteşe in southwest Anatolia was founded by Menteşe Bey, an Oghuz Turk. The Menteşe Emirate had ruled Caria for more than a hundred years when the Ottoman Turks, on the ascendancy but not yet in Constantinople, turned their attention south. In return for their assistance against Tamerlane, the knights were allowed to build a castle in Bodrum.

In 1402, the Menteşe fortifications, which had been built

over the acropolis on the island of Zephyros, were greatly enlarged under the Order's Grand Master, the French knight Philibert de Naillac. The architect was Heinrich Schlegelholdt, who described how they had "torn down, smashed and burned" (to make lime for mortar) the ruins of the Mausoleum for use in their project. The German knight devised the five towers and seven gates, and included five cisterns to stand any lengthy siege. He was also responsible for building the large castle on the island of Kos opposite, to control the shipping lanes around this corner of Anatolia.

Bodrum castle served the knights for little more than a century. The Turks were on the march. The Christian Byzantine Empire was shrinking under successive waves of attacks, but it was not until seventy years after the fall of Constantinople that Anatolia was completely overrun, and the knights driven from Bodrum and the islands by Süleyman the Magnificent, who gathered a fleet in the harbour at Marmaris to take Rhodes. The defeated knights left for Malta. Focused entirely on their crusading zeal, they left behind no single mark of civilising activity. The Castle of St Peter, known to the Ottomans as Petrion, was corrupted into Bodrum, the new name of the town. (It is also the Turkish for 'basement', *bodrum katı* meaning the 'basement floor' of a building.) The castle remained a bastion against piracy and attack and its chapel was replaced by a mosque. A hammam was installed and no foreigners were allowed inside its walls.

Francis Beaufort, who arrived in 'Boodroom' in 1812 to start his survey of the coast, told the story of the commander of a French frigate who a few years earlier had asked to see the marbles from the Mausoleum known to be in the castle. The governor told him that he could only let him in if he had direct orders from the Porte. So the frigate sailed to Constantinople where, via the French ambassador, he obtained the necessary permission, a *ferman*. On being presented with this, the castle governor touched it to his head as a mark of obeisance to the higher authority, and turned towards the outer gate where he stopped and said, "*Efendi*, the orders of my imperial master must be implicitly obeyed."

"Let me in, then," the French Captain snapped impatiently.

"Undoubtedly," the Turk replied, "for so I am enjoined to do by the *ferman*, but as it contains no directions as to your coming out again, you will perhaps forgive this momentary pause before we cross the drawbridge."

The Frenchman fled.

Cevat Şakir must have been resigned to his fate in this distant bastion, to crossing the drawbridge and being let in, and for three years not coming out. If he wrote a letter to his wife, it might be half a year before he received a reply. From a cell shared with bandits and dissidents, the castle would not hold the romance that it had done for antiquarians. But he might have expected some lively conversations, from bandits, deserters or spies, or with the leaders of an Islamic fundamentalist revolt, who before the war had been sentenced to life imprisonment in the castle.

He might also have wondered if he would ever reach Bodrum at all. Stopping at town prisons along the way, the 700-km journey from Ankara across wild and untramelled country took three months to complete. An escort of two gendarmes was supposed to ensure safe delivery. Had the local bandits known the prisoner's family connections, they might have queued up to kidnap him at every pass. But news travelled slowly in these remote parts, if it travelled at all.

What Cevat Şakir found when he finally reached the castle was a surprise. It was a surprise to the local authorities, too. When the gendarmes handed over the paperwork from the court with details of the sentence, the lone local policeman had to explain that the castle was no longer in use as a prison. The last prisoners had left ten years earlier when the castle had been bombarded by the French. Like Pascali's, the governor's reports to the capital had gone unread. So while the two gendarmes turned around and prepared for the arduous slog homewards, suggesting a sequel that had all the hallmarks of another *Rosencrantz and Guildenstern*, the policeman and Cevat Şakir were left scratching their heads wondering what to do. There was only one solution, of course. The prisoner would have to be housed in the town, and since he seemed such an engaging chap, potential good company on long winter evenings, a one-room whitewashed stone house was found for him, right by the sea.

"*When I opened my door,*" Cevat Şakir wrote of his first day in his new home, "*I saw the sunset over the sea and the scarlet rays of the dying sun falling on the shores and the islands…. As if in a religious ecstasy I fell on my knees and felt my spirit rising out of my inanimate body like a million twittering birds.*"

And so the exile of the Fisherman of Halicarnassus began.

5. CORSAIRS, KINGS OF THE SEA

For those who know of Homer, it is impossible to sail in Blue Voyage waters without wondering if Odysseus's galley might come into view, or if the peace won't suddenly be disturbed by Poseidon, 'Lord of the earthquakes, god of the sable locks', who ruled the tempestuous seas as Zeus ruled the skies. There might be pirates, too. At any moment a bowsprit might appear, a sail, a salvo, to herald trouble or deliverance, depending on whose side they were on. Today's Blue Voyagers might conjure characters from the Caribbean, but Cevat Şakir recalled the great days of the Ottoman Empire, when Süleyman the Magnificent was extending its land borders, and his Grand Admirals Barbarossa and Dragut were kings of the sea.

The sudden sight of a fleet of Barbary corsairs would set every Christian heart racing, as it did the Knights of St John on the island of Malta one May morning in 1565. It had been less than fifty years since the Order's Grand Master had knelt humiliatingly at the feet of Süleyman the Magnificent in Rhodes and kissed his hand, accepting defeat and banishment from all the Order's castles around the Turkish coast. Now they were under siege again, in their new base in Malta. The strategic island on the narrowest part of the Mediterranean that separates it east from west had been a gift, along with Tripoli, from Holy Roman Emperor Charles V, King of Spain, Naples and Sicily. *"Take these and defend them with your lives,"* he may well have said, "*and while you are at it drive the Turks to the bottom of the sea.*" Süleyman regretted letting the knights free to cause havoc on Ottoman shipping, and in 1565 he finally launched an attack on the island. In his classic tale, *The Great Siege*, the English author-sailor Ernle Bradford described the appearance of Süleyman's greatest admiral, following the arrival of the main Ottoman fleet:

"*It was at that moment that the sentries noticed the other ships approaching from the southeast. The word went round: 'It is Dragut!' It was known, from runaways and captured prisoners, that the great corsair had been expected ever since the beginning of the siege. There could be no doubt that this squadron of fifteen ships approaching from North Africa was Dragut's, the greatest Moslem seaman of his time.*"

Dragut was eighty years old and had spent a lifetime building his reputation. Corsair, privateer, galley slave, naval commander, Governor of the Mediterranean, Pasha, his life was as colourful and full of incident and derring-do as any seaborne adventurer's. Today he is celebrated as a hero in Turkey and Algeria, and paraded as a villainous figure at festivals in ports and resorts around Italy and Spain. Cruelty and courage were the necessary attributes of heroic 16th-century sailors. Faint hearts never won empires, and Dragut played a significant role in the expanding the Ottoman Empire throughout Süleyman the Magnificent's forty-six-year reign. It was also a world of fast-changing fortunes. At the age of fifty Dragut had been captured and put to work in Genoan galleys for four years, before taking over from Hayreddin Barbarossa, Süleyman's famous naval commander, on his retirement.

Barbarossa was seven years older than Dragut and they remained close all their lives, Barbarossa's son marrying Dragut's daughter. But the affinity that the two men felt began with their birthplaces on the Aegean: Barbarossa in 1478 at

Mytilene on the island of Lesvos, not long taken from its Genoese occupiers, and Dragut in the fishing village of Karatoprak on the Bodrum peninsula just over 200 kilometres to the south. The real name of Barbarossa ("Red Beard") was Khizir, later also called Kheir-ed-Din, Protector of Religion, and he was the youngest of four sons and two daughters, of an Ottoman soldier. Tradition has it that his mother was a Christian and his father a Muslim convert. His oldest brother, Oruç had been seized by the Knights of St John while sailing the Lycian coast with his younger brother Isaac, trading and perhaps doing a little pirating. One calm day *Our Lady of Conception*, canvases blazing with white crosses, appeared around a headland, the knight-captain high on the poop deck beneath a damask canopy embroidered in gold. With a greater number of oarsmen, she bore down Oruç, firing her cannons before there was a chance to surrender, and killing Isaac. Along with the surviving crew, Oruç was condemned as a galley slave for several years before being ransomed. The story spread along the coast to Dragut's village where Oruç and his brothers had sometimes stopped on their trips around the coast.

The Fisherman of Halicarnassus contemplated such a meeting when he was writing *Turgut Reis* (*Captain Dragut*; Turgut is the Turkish form of Dragut), his novel about the sailor published in 1966. Turgut is a common name among Oghuz Turks, who came from around the Turgai valley in central Asia, so Dragut defies the perception of Turks as plainsmen who preferred horses to boats, the saddle to the paddle. This thought was in Cevat Şakir's mind when he contemplated this hero of Anatolia, whose talent was recognised as much among Christian sailors as among Muslims. The respected 19th-century French naval historian Admiral Edmond Jurien de la Gravière wrote:

"*Dragut was superior to Barbarossa. A living chart of the*

Mediterranean, he combined science with audacity. There was not a creek unknown to him, not a channel that he had not sailed. Ingenious in devising ways and means, when all around him despaired, he excelled above all in escaping by unprecedented methods from situations of great peril. An incomparable pilot, he had no equal in sea warfare except the chevalier Romegas [Mathurin d'Aux de Lescout Romegas, General of the Galleys in Malta]. *On land he was skilful enough to be compared with the finest generals of Charles V and Philip II. He had known the hardship of captivity and he showed himself humane to his own captives. Under every aspect he was a character. No one was more worthy than he to bear the title of 'King'..."*

The victories that Dragut, 'the sword of Islam', won at sea complemented the advances of Süleyman. The Ottoman Empire now extended through the Middle East to Egypt and the Persian Gulf, and north through Belgrade to the very gates of Vienna. But Ottoman expansion in the East came at a time of the Muslim contraction in the West, with the defeat of the Emirate of Granada. Expelled from Spain and given just a few days to leave their homes, Jews and Muslims of Al-Andalus flooded onto the Mediterranean's southern shore – the Barbary coast named after the Berber tribes. Following the death of the Prophet Muhammad nearly nine centuries earlier, the faithful had sped west to spread the word: now they were heading the other way. Barbarossa and his brother Oruç aided in this evacuation, and they saw it their duty to try to prevent the Christian forces following up the advances they had made on the Iberian peninsula by invading North Africa.

A condition of Barbarossa's appointment as admiral of the Ottoman fleet had been that he handed over his personally acquired territory to the Sultan, including Algiers, the most important North African port. A contemporary Spanish account describes this "den of thieves" as being stuffed full of

45

gold, silver, pearls, amber, spices, drugs, silks and velvets, making it "the most opulent city in the world".

The Mediterranean was a ceaseless battleground of Christian and Muslim ships. Corsairs had successfully taken a number of Aegean and Ionian islands held by the Genoese and Venetians, and were plundering the ports of southern Italy. Trade, particularly for the Venetians, was severely affected, and in 1538 the Pope convened a Holy League of Western Mediterranean states to combat the advance of Islam. The result was the first full-scale clash of the Mediterranean's seaborne nations. The papal fleet, under the Genoan admiral Andrea Doria, tracked down Barbarossa off the coast of northwest Greece. Battle was engaged at Preveza on September 29, and though outnumbered, the Ottomans, with Dragut leading a vanguard of speedy galliots, won the day.

The subsequent peace treaty gave Süleyman the Venetian possessions in the Peloponnese, as well as most of the remaining islands of the Aegean, Ionian and Adriatic. For more than three decades much of the Mediterranean was in Ottoman control, largely due to the Bodrum commander and the Barbary corsairs.

That did not mean they had it all their own way. Two years after the battle of Preveza, Dragut was in Corsica where his ships' hulls were having their regular cleaning, when he was unexpectedly surrounded by Genoan forces led by Gianettino Doria, the nephew of Admiral Andrea, who was delighted with such a prize. For the next four years, up until the age of sixty, Dragut was a galley slave, shackled to a bench and for a time under the lash on the admiral's own flagship. Among those who recognised the prisoner was Jean Parisot de Valette, Chevalier of the Langue de Provence, who had himself spent a year as a corsair galley slave. He reportedly acknowledged his foe sympathetically with the words: "It's just the customs of war", to which Dragut replied, "Yes, and the changes of fortune." At times like that, the Mediterranean must have seemed a small pond.

Dragut was finally ransomed for 3,000 crowns by Barabarossa, who put the highest value on his worth. On his release, Dragut went back to business, attacking Christian shipping from a base on Djerba, North Africa's largest island, which lies off the east coast of Tunisia southwest of Malta. From here he could harass the grain cargoes from Sicily, so vital to the region. He and his corsairs were also able to take Tripoli from the Knights of St John. Dragut set about transforming it into a prosperous city, fortifying it, building a mosque and creating a palace for himself in which, after Barbarossa retired from the sea aged seventy-seven, he took over the role as *pasha*.

In his robes, dripping with jewellery, with an arsenal of pearl-handled daggers and scimitars encrusted with opals, rubies and turquoise, striding through cool tiled halls between courtyard fountains, Dragut would have been a princely sight. But he was uninterested in the comforts of life and was more often in his naval base at Djerba. It was here that Andrea Doria once more sought him out, in 1560, catching him by surprise and blocking the entrance to the lagoon where Dragut's ships were beached for cleaning and re-tarring. The Ottoman admiral's response was to cut a channel through a causeway into the open sea – some say he dragged his boats overland, *à la* Fitzcaraldo. Either way, he made his escape from right under Doria's nose, enhancing his reputation as a slippery character and master of strategy.

Unfortunately for the Ottomans, Dragut was not in charge of the navy when the siege of Malta was planned. Although he had a raft of exalted titles, and was deferred to in most military matters, Dragut never achieved the post that Barbarossa had held as admiral of the fleet. Instead the job went to Piyale Pasha, who was married to Süleyman's granddaughter. By the time Dragut had been spotted coming into view from the Barbary coast, the bulk of the Ottoman forces of some 40,000 soldiers and sailors from 193 ships was already at the foot of the island's fortress of St Elmo. The knights were now under the command of Jean de Valette, who as a young knight had witnessed the humiliation of the Order at Rhodes.

Dragut knew Malta and its sister island of Gozo well. Little more than a dozen years earlier he had raided Gozo and removed, so it is said, its entire population of 5,000 into slavery in North Africa. But as he and the island's defender Jean de Valette, who would give his name to the island's capital, Valetta, both knew, the fortunes of war can change on an instant. Dragut's moment had come. Always a hands-on commander, he was setting up a new battery when a cannon ball shattered the rock overhead sending shards in every direction. One of these penetrated his turban, piercing his skull. He died six days later and his remains were taken to Tripoli, a town that could be called his own. There it was placed in a low, green sarcophagus in the inner court of the Dragut Pasha mosque, which he had built. It remains a place of pilgrimage today.

There is also statue of him in Karatoprak, a smart resort of opulent motorboats and yachts that would be unrecognisable to both Dragut, its most famous son, and to Cevat Şakir. But the Fisherman of Halicarnassus lived just long enough to see the town's name changed to Turgutreis in recognition of his sailor hero who for so long ruled the seas.

6. SPONGE DIVERS

When Cevat Şakir Kabaağaçli arrived in Bodrum in 1925, he might have expected to see a few walking wounded from the First World War and from the subsequent fight to save Turkey – men without limbs, perhaps, or without sight, or scarred by bayonets, bullets or blasts. But on the quayside, in the cafés or among the alleys pungent with the smell of drying sponges, he also saw men with a kind of injury he had never witnessed before: men crippled by decompression sickness, which left them unable to walk, or with convulsions, a lack of muscle co-ordination, incontinence, sensory abnormalities, numbness, or speech defects.

Sponge diving had been carried on in the area since the dawn of civilisation, but it was only since diving suits had replaced natural skin diving that the bends had become a hazard of the industry. Breathing under pressure increases the amount of nitrogen in the body's tissues, which remains in solution until the pressure is relaxed, and if it is relaxed too quickly, the nitrogen gassifies, its bubbles attacking the joints, the bendy bits of the body, causing the "bends". It felt like a beating, and in Turkish it is called *vurgun yemek*, meaning 'taking a punch'.

The result was both debilitating and incurable. The Fisherman described one paralised old sponge diver, nicknamed 'Grandpa Crab', who said: "My paralysis is only on land. On the sea floor I'm like a bird, a balloon."

Little was known about the bends at the time, and the riches brought by the new invention came at a terrible price. In the two decades following the introduction of diving suits and air pumps in the 1880s, the death toll in the Aegean and Ottoman islands was shocking. Over the following twenty-five years, 10,000 Mediterranean divers were lost and 20,000 permanently disabled, according to Faith Worn author of *Bitter Sea: the real story of Greek sponge diving*.

As a result of these disasters, widows and grieving mothers petitioned the Sultan, who granted their pleas, and put a ban on the use of air-pump assisted dives. But this led to a dramatic loss of income, and it wasn't long before the suits were being pulled on again.

Local sources of sponge, this strange animal that grows in colonies where it can feed off passing currents, could not meet demands, and fleets began to venture further afield. The most lucrative waters were off North Africa where a lack of ports meant the sponge boats would spend months at sea, moving up and down the coast. Any victim of the bends might be put ashore where he would find some relief from the pain by being buried up to his neck in hot sand and left with a comrade until the boat returned a few days later, by which time either the pain would have abated, or he would be dead.

Each spring boats would put to sea for the season, taking with them young lads from the countryside with the promise of riches, a dozen or more of them packed tight as sardines on the boat, eating one meal a day, in the evening, to keep their weight down. The Fisherman describes them crammed on deck to sleep beneath the moon, *"resembling dead and wounded soldiers lined up on the battlefield after the battle is over"*. As days turned into weeks and months, those left behind wondered if they would ever return. As in a Greek tragedy, women would replace their white headscarves with black ones until their menfolk were safely home.

Just off Bodrum peninsula is the island of Kalymnos, historically the centre of sponge diving in the Mediterranean. Visiting in 1952, Lawrence Durrell described the *"poetic fatality – so ancient Greek in its vividness"* that came over its harbour just before the fleet set sail for Libya. *"The sight was unforgettable, worthy of some great classical painter....the tension in the air, the pain of leave taking, the heavy weight of the absence to be borne, the uncertainties and dangers to be encountered... everything was marked on the faces of the silent women. They were still and undemonstrative as leaves."*

At that time decompression chambers were only just being introduced. The American diver Peter Throckmorton, who spent many months among Bodrum's sponge divers in the late 1950s, describes the death of an old and experienced diver, and his frustration at not being able to get him to the nearest decompression chamber – in Istanbul.

In 1959 Throckmorton pioneered in Bodrum what came to be called the *nargile* diving technique, named after the Turkish hookah or waterpipe. This used an air tube from an on-board pump, which was adjusted by a regulator on the diver's back. Instead of full diving gear, the diver wore mask and flippers. It meant the diver could spend a long time on the seabed, but it still required a slow and sensible ascent to the surface. Divers knew the risks, and the symptoms, but they did not have decompression tables. They lived by their experience and by knowledge handed down. Death was never far away, but the divers were proud of their work, and those who were damaged were treated with respect.

The rewards must have been worthwhile to keep such a way of life going, a life that had no global boundaries. Early in the 20th century, sailors from Kalymnos and neighbouring

Symi had emigrated to the US to start a major sponge industry in Florida and the Gulf of Mexico, based in Tarpon Springs. After the Second World War they took the place of Japanese pearl divers in Australia.

The Fisherman of Halicarnassus wrote several stories describing the lives of Bodrum's sponge fishermen. In 'The Aegean Floor' a steamer from Marmaris sinks in Izmir Bay. Among the passengers that go down with the ship is a businessman with all his and his partner's money. Ashore in Ayvalık, the partner heads for Bodrum and the Yalı café to find Alish of Marmaris, 'the Sea Wolf' who "strolls about in fifty fathoms as though he's walking in the street". Reluctant at first, Alish is persuaded by increased offers of payment. There is no doubt about the dangers he faces as he puts on his diving gear to search among the shark-nibbled bodies in the cabins of the sunken vessel.

Always ready to take up the sponge fishermen's cause, the Fisherman helped to overturn a ban on the *gangava*. This was a catch-all net winched up and down by the boat's engine. It was attached to an eight-metre axle with an iron wheel at each end and a threshing chain that trawled the sea bed (one can be seen in the grounds of Bodrum Castle). It tore the sponges up by their roots and damaged any archaeological remains, but it avoided the need for deep dives and the possibilities of the bends. Cevat Şakir did not live to see the ban reinstated, two years after his death.

Sponges are dark, shiny organisms, round or conical, formed from the waste product of protoplasm. The skeleton has a similar chemical make-up to silk. Taken from the seabed, they were traditionally pressed on deck either by treading on them or beating them with sticks to rid them of extraneous material, a job for the young lads. They were then cleaned in nets thrown overboard before being pummelled again and left to dry in the sun until all that remained was their skeleton of 'spongin', which would be shaped and trimmed with a knife.

First mention of sponges comes to us from Homer who describes their use by Odysseus's servants to swab tables clean, and by the smithy Hephaistos to wipe the grime from his limbs. Opianus, a 2nd-century poet from Cilicia in eastern Anatolia, wrote, "*As for the work of sponge cutters, I declare there is none worse, nor any work more woeful for man.*" Sponge formed a padding for armour in Classical times, and the Romans used sponges on sticks to act as lavatory paper. Doused in lemon juice, sponges were employed as a prophylactic in the Sultan's harem, as well as by some Bodrum villagers up until the 1960s before modern contraception was introduced.

During the heyday of La Serenissima, the Venetians had a monopoly of the Mediterranean trade and sponges were called *venetias*. The fine Honeycomb sponge, best for bathrooms, is still called *venise* in French. By the 19th century the general distribution point for all European and Asiatic sponges had crossed the Adriatic from Venice to Habsburg Trieste – "*whence come the delicate Turkish sponges so indispensable to my lady's toilet and invaluable to surgeons*," reports *Scribner's* magazine of 1892, a time when Aegean islands were still Ottoman owned. Only a few of the many species of sponge are suitable for domestic use. Fine Turkey Cup (very soft), Fine Turkey Solid (cushion-shaped, for the bath) and Brown Turkey (disc shaped, for scrubbing) are all well-known varieties, as is Honeycomb and Elephant's Ear (useful for stuffing and polishing).

Synthetic sponges, invented in 1942 by the DuPont company, put paid to much of the industry, as did the war and a post-war fishing ban on foreign vessels imposed by Egypt and Libya. By the 1960s, there was only a handful of sponge fishing boats in the town. Then, in 1987, sponges throughout the Mediterranean were infected with a blight, which recurred in the 1990s.

The sponges that snorkelling divers find around the coast today are hardly worth disturbing. Sponge fishing has become just a part of Bodrum's history, celebrated in its museums and monuments. Most of the small sponges bought from street sellers or in souvenir shops are imported. In the harbour a small sponge boat, painted Aegean blue and dwarfed by the gulets, displays a defiant notice saying that it will carry on the age-old tradition. It is called *Aksona*, the name of Bodrum's most famous sponge diver, Aksona Mehmet, who has long campaigned for the revival of sponge fishing in the town.

Although the industry has run its course in Turkey, it still operates in Greece, and in 2004 sponges were given to all the participants in the Athens Olympic Games where it was proposed that Skandalopetra Free Diving become an Olympic sport. Skandalopetra takes its name from the traditional stone weight, usually around 15kg, which a diver would use to steer him into depths of up to thirty metres. (Divers were invariably 'he', with the exception of Sophia Loren, who played a ravishing but poor Greek sponge diver in the 1957 film *Boy on a Dolphin*.) The stone had a hole through which a rope was attached to guide him and his catch back to the boat. Skandaloptera failed to make it onto the XXVIII Olympiad programme, but it has become an established sport, with annual championships held in Kalymnos and around the world.

Meanwhile the art of deep diving is still very much alive in Turkey. Free diving championships are held around Bodrum and around Kaş off the Lycian coast where the limestone Taurus mountains plunge deep into the peerless sea. With the aid of large flippers, the fittest can reach depths of around 120 metres, nearly twice that of traditional sponge divers. Turkish world record breakers such as Yasemin Dalkılıç and Şahika Ercümen have also shown that women would have been just as successful sponge divers as men. If only this had been recognised in the time of Homer, and women had been sponge divers, too, the history of the industry might have been quite different.

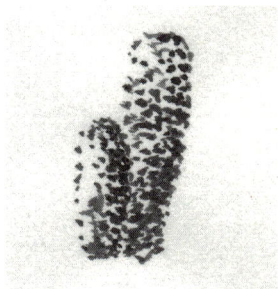

7. UNDERWATER ARCHAEOLOGY

"I can still hear Cevat Bey's booming '*Mer-ha-ba*', very carefully pronounced as three distinct syllables," recalls George Bass, who had been warned that this was how the Fisherman of Halicarnassus was likely to greet him when they were introduced by Peter Throckmorton. The American diver had imitated the impending Turkish greeting in a way Bass describes as "dead on".

Bodrum is where the science of underwater archaeology began, and Dr George F. Bass is its founding father. Now Professor of Nautical Archaeology at Texas A&M University, he has a number of awards and medals, and in 2012 he was elected a Fellow of the American Academy of Arts and Sciences. He also set up the first organisation devoted to underwater archaeology, the Institute of Nautical Archaeology, whose headquarters in Bodrum was purpose-built beside the house he still uses when visiting.

It was 1960 when he arrived in the port, by which time The Fisherman was living in Izmir.

"I know of no influence Cevat Bey had on underwater archaeology in Bodrum," he says, "except that he did show interest in it and appreciation for it when I met him very briefly on his trips by sea to Bodrum with his Istanbul friends. I knew of his time spent in Bodrum and that he was a beloved author. My Turkish after half a century of working out of Bodrum is still not good enough to read a novel in Turkish, so

I hope some of his writing is one day translated into English."

Cevat Şakir had heard fishermen's accounts about finds in the sea, though these were not generally spoken of in wonder and amazement, but rather as complaints of hazards and nuisances. This was an exceptionally busy corner of the Mediterranean, and ships had been rounding the coast day and night since man first put to sea, carrying whatever they could to make a living. Staying in sight of land, a high percentage of vessels trading between the Middle East and Europe would have passed by, making the most of the shelter of the coast and islands. There were many islets, rocks and reefs to navigate, many storms to ride, and it is generally on the capes that they came to grief. Before the invention of the diving suit and *gangava*, the seabed around Bodrum must have looked like a deserted city, with blocks of cargoes, avenues of ships' timbers and fields of amphorae. Skin divers would by and large leave them alone, cutting sponges from their encrusted surfaces and not taking any notice of anything that lay beyond the depths that their breaths would take them.

When the air pumps were introduced it was a different matter. Anything that hindered the path of a heavy-booted diver was a nuisance, and relics caught in nets that trawled the bed were either smashed to pieces in the process or brought to the surface and destroyed so they would cause no further damage. Boxes, once opened and proved to contain nothing useful were thrown away. Metal objects such as bronze cannon and lead anchors would be melted for scrap, and anything larger that caused an obstruction was liable to have been dynamited. In shops, amphorae could be bought for virtually nothing, and there are tales of sponge divers destroying up to fifty in a single day.

Any thoughts that Turkey's seabed might have held anything worth more than its scrap value first surfaced in 1953 when an eighty-centimetre bronze bust of Demeter was discovered and put on display at the archaeological museum in Izmir. The statue had been dredged up in a *gangava* from a boat owned by Mehmet Erbil, a sponge fisherman from Bodrum. He and his crew had been working off Arap Adasi, a point on the Bozburun peninsula south of Marmaris.

Back in Bodrum it wasn't given much attention and was left lying on a beach where it was spotted and identified as a work from the 4th century BC by George Bean, a British archaeologist attached to Istanbul University. He had it sent to the museum in Izmir where it was cleaned and put on display. Larger than life-size, the goddess of corn, popular in Anatolia, was heavily dressed, although only the upper torso remained, and the back of the head had disappeared. It had not been cast as one piece, but in small sections welded together. The story caught the imagination round the world, and Bean, the author of four seminal guide books to the sites of antiquity in coastal Turkey, wrote an article about its importance for the *Illustrated London News*.

Many authorities date the start of underwater archaeology to the Bodrum Demeter, but it was not the first find in the Aegean. In 1900 a sponge diver from Symi stumbled on a massive pile of cargo off the island of Antikythera northwest of Crete, dating from around the time of Julius Caesar. The haul of marble and bronze statuary, furniture, jewellery, ceramics and the first known computer, the brass Antikythera Mechanism, was apparently a job lot of Greek goods from Rhodes that had been bought by a rich Roman and was on its way to being delivered. The Greek navy hauled up what they could at the time, and in 1976 Jacques Cousteau and his famous dive ship *Calypso* took another look, but only a few scraps of wood from the ship bearing the cargo were ever found.

It was Cousteau's invention of the aqualung that propelled a post-war generation of divers to scour the seabeds. And it was Demeter who beckoned Peter Throckmorton towards Bodrum. Despite his pre-eminence in the world of underwater archaeology, Professor Bass is quick to credit his fellow American for starting it all.

Born in New York, Throckmorton had been interested in the sea and shipwrecks since he was a child, and he recalls collecting marine debris in Long Island in 1938, aged nine, following a great storm. Rejected by the navy because of poor eyesight, he worked on all kinds of boats, learned to dive and signed up with the army, who sent him to the Yokohama shipyard. The same year that the aqualung came out, he enrolled at the University of Hawaii where, to earn pennies, he dived for tourists, spending his spare time among wrecks. Still on the GI Bill, at the age of twenty-five he was accepted for a higher degree in ethnology at the Musée de l'Homme in Paris. Here he took up with a documentary film maker and became a freelance photo-journalist, travelling around Europe and Asia and failing to finish his course.

In late 1957, after photographing a tiger hunt in India for *Argosy* magazine, he was returning to Paris via Afghanistan when he found himself in Istanbul, which is where he came across the story of Demeter. His diving enthusiasm rekindled, he immediately decided to head for Bodrum and seek out Captain Mehmet Erbil to direct him to the spot where the statue had been netted in the hope that other treasures might be lying nearby. First stop, however, was the museum in Izmir. Here he saw Demeter, displayed in a glass case, and met with the museum's director, Hakkı Gültekin, a colleague of Bean's, who had followed up the original find with further exploration by Turkey's first underwater photographer, Mustafa Kapkin, but nothing more had turned up.

Throckmorton met Kapkin and they hit it off, and together they went to try to find out what else might be lying in the waters around Bodrum. Captain Erbil, however, had put to sea for the season, and was no longer in Bodrum, but being strangers in town they didn't have to ask too many questions before another sponge boat captain, Kemal Aras, was telling them about wrecks he had seen beneath the sea, particularly off an island called Yassi Ada where the abundance of amphorae made it difficult to work. That summer, Throckmorton and Kapkin with Kemal and his crew dived as nobody had dived there before, with equipment that the American introduced, not without a large degree of frustration caused by unhelpful customs officers.

In the end they were to identify three particular wrecks, from the 4th, 7th and 16th centuries, all of which would eventually be properly excavated. The Byzantine wreck from the 7th century was deemed particularly important as it showed a stage of developments in shipbuilding between ancient and modern.

Returning to Bodrum the following year, Throckmorton discovered that, in response to his appeal, local fishermen had collected so many amphorae and other items from the seabed that it was hard to know where to put them. In *The Lost Ships*, his book about the two years he spent diving in Bodrum, he recalls:

"Hakkı Bey had a long talk with Osman Bey, the director of education in Bodrum, and received his permission to use the Knights' Hall of the Crusaders' castle as a storeroom. It was the only building in the castle that had a real door. Kemal dug around in his back yard, found a couple of amphoras, and hauled them up to the castle. Plaster was peeling off the walls in sheets, and choking

*clouds of dust and dried mule dung rose when we scuffed our feet.
It didn't matter. It was a museum, and it was ours."*

At the end of the season, he heard about some half a dozen
large bronze ingots that Kemal had found off Cape Gelidonya
on the southeast coast of Lycia, and when he learned that
Kemal planned to dynamite the site the following spring, he
persuaded the captain to hold off till he had a chance to
excavate it. But if this really was the important site that he
hoped it might be, it would need proper professional
archaeologists, ones who were prepared to do what no other
archaeologist had done before: excavate a site underwater.

Back in the US, Throckmorton was steered towards the
archaeology department of the University of Pennsylvania
where George Bass was adding a PhD in Classical archaeology
to the MA in Near Eastern Archaeology he had gained from
Johns Hopkins University. He also had field experience of
excavations in Greece and Turkey, and as a GI in Korea had
been in charge of a US army unit imbedded in a Turkish
brigade. He had never dived before, but he was game, and
after half a dozen lessons in the local YMCA pool, he and
Throckmorton headed for Bodrum, where, Bass recalls, "There
were more camels than trucks."

The summer was spent encamped on a beach near Cape
Gelidonya. George Bass directed the operations, Hakkı
Gültekin ensured Turkish interests were met and the artist
Honor Frost made all-important drawings of the wreck. She
had studied at the Slade and at Ruskin College Oxford,
discovered diving in Cannes and recorded archaeological digs
in Jericho and the Middle East, where she began to realise the
importance of proper scientific methods and how they might
be applied to underwater finds. Her work at Cape Gelidonya
confirmed that the vessel Kemal was about to blow up dated
from 1200BC. Bass concluded it was from the Near East,

which meant a re-setting of the historical clock to an earlier time of vessels trading in copper and tin, the minerals that made bronze, than had hitherto been thought.

'The Oldest Shipwreck Ever Found' was the cover story of *National Geographic* in May 1960, with colour photos of the dives by Throckmorton. The finds also sparked a call for a proper museum to be established in the castle. Hakkı Gültekin put pressure on the government and a national newspaper campaign was led by Cevat Şakir's Blue Voyage companion Azra Erhat.

The result was the creation of the Bodrum Museum in 1961 and the gradual restoration of the castle. Today the museum has an unparalleled collection of underwater archaeology, and the names of George Bass and Texas A&M University are much in evidence, as are their finds from Yassi Ada and Cape Gelidonya.

In 1982 a sponge diver encountered an even older and more spectacular wreck for George Bass and his team to excavate. The 24-metre Uluburun ship had a cargo of copper ingots from mines in Cyprus, and during eleven seasons of excavations more than 18,000 objects were brought to the surface, including Egyptian jewellery and vessels of ivory and gold. Built of cedar wood and oak, this proved to be a royal ship from 1400BC. The *National Geographic*'s report on the find ran to four dozen pages.

The not-for-profit Institute of Nautical Archaeology, which Bass set up in 1973, has its Mediterranean headquarters on the hills overlooking Bodrum, and a global reach. The neo-Ottoman complex behind one of the last surviving stretches of Mausolos's city wall includes dormitories, laboratories, offices, conservation facilities and libraries. Salvaged material needs years of treatment in tanks of water and chemicals, and the Institute is currently looking at eight of thirty ships from the 5th to 10th centuries discovered in 2004 in Istanbul. This extraordinary haul from the hitherto unknown port at Yenikapı is the largest to date and was discovered while the rail tunnel under the Bosphorus to link the European and Asian shores was being excavated.

INA's own ship and a submersible constantly monitor wrecks in Turkey, though the debate about whether to allow accredited dive schools and clubs access to the sites as a means of policing them is a matter of continuing debate.

Among the books is in the INA library is a collection from Peter Throckmorton, who continued his interest in underwater archaeology in sites around the world. The two years he had spent with the divers in Bodrum had been intense, his battles with the authorities arduous, and diving with the sponge boats exhausting. As one of the village's first resident foreigners he was always open to scrutiny, and seldom left alone, even when in his own room.

He died in 1990 and left his books to the library, where there was already a copy of *The Lost Ships*, published in 1964, his engaging story of that extraordinary time he spent among the sponge divers that Cevat Şakir knew. Though he was living in Izmir by then, the Fisherman still spent his summers in Bodrum, greeting Thockmorton, and everyone else, with his characteristic *"Mer-ha-ba*!"

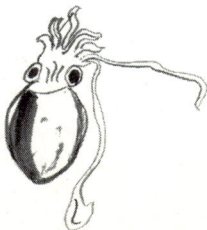

8. GULETS AND TIRHANDILS

On the third week of October each year, at the end of the cruising season, scores of Blue Cruise yachts take part in the five-day Bodrum Cup. It is one of the few major regattas in the world that allows chartered boats to participate, so anyone can hitch a ride. Friends and family come along, too, and the captains and crews, who all summer long have been polite to their guests and kept their boats on steady courses, now put their skills to the test, pitting their vessels and skills against each other along the coast and around the neighbouring islands. It is a last jubilant burst of energy before the boats are lifted out of the water for their winter overhaul.

Despite this desertion from the quaysides, Bodrum harbour still somehow looks fully occupied. In fact it is hard to imagine a port anywhere in the world with such a collection of traditional wooden sailing boats. They make up a good part of the 3,500 motor vessels registered in the port, their highly varnished timbers creaking fender-to-fender along the quays and jetties, and their tidy decks and appealing lines attesting to Turkish seamanship and boat-building skills. With all the comforts of a modern hotel, with awnings and sofas, generous dining tables, masterly helms and inviting gangplanks, they can look so alike that passengers may take a little while to locate the one they have just left.

They are a world away from *Yatağan*, the sponge divers' tirhandil that the Fisherman of Halicarnassus bought for his early voyages. During his exile, his punishment included a ban on putting to sea, and all he could do was watch from the shore as the fishing and sponge boats set sail for their catches. After a frustrating eighteen months he was sent to Constantinople to complete his prison term, but as soon as he was released he returned to Bodrum and bought the boat that would be associated with his name. Yatağan is the name of both a short Ottoman sword and an inland town where pines are cut for boat building, which was named after the Fisherman's tirhandil. Today the town is known for its annual camel wrestling matches and its coal-fired power plant.

The 7.5-metre gaff-rigged open boat was in fact built in Greece, and a model of it can be seen in the Bodrum Maritime Museum, along with many others that show the different styles of vessels that have ploughed the Gulf of Gökova since the second half of the 20th century.

They are all variations of caiques (*kayık* in Turkish) and ketches, and probably no two are alike. The main features of a tirhandil (from the Greek *trehandíri*) are a curved bow with a bowsprit and near vertical, pointed stern with a large rudder and tiller arm, and a profile that swoops down towards the midships where the gunwales are close to the water. It is three times the length of its beam. Easily beached, tirhandils are wide with a shallow draft, and were originally lanteen or gaff rigged, sometimes with a staysail, though contemporary models are sloop rigged with a single mast. They handled in all weathers and were easily manoeuvred, making them the boat of choice for sponge skin divers. They provided simple accommodation with decks that could be slept on, and they were also used to carry produce around the shores and islands of the Aegean and Mediterranean seas.

From out of the tirhandil came the gulet, Bodrum's singular gift to the sailing world, its semi-circular stern cut away, its bow concave, 'clipper' style, and its lanteen sail replaced by a schooner rig. In fact, according to local expert Timuçin Binder, gulet is a word borrowed from the French *goélette* and the Italian *goletta*, and it describes the schooner (*uskuna*) rigging rather than the hull shape. This means two masts of almost equal height, a mainsail, mizen and a jib or three, plus the ability to hoist a spinnaker. A variant on the gulet is the *ayna kiç*, which has a square stern, allowing for a broad rear cabin with windows looking out over the wake. This kind of boat is sometimes called a 'mirror-aft' or 'panelled' gulet, and sometimes it is just called a ketch.

The modern story of tirhandils and gulets began at the end of the 19th and start of the 20th century with the arrival of Cretan refugees who brought their boat-building traditions with them. Though boats were undoubtedly built to replace those lost in the attack on the port in 1915, experts at Bodrum Maritime Museum trace their history only as far back as 1933 when a Greek immigrant, Nami'nin Mehmet (Mehmet of Nami), built a tirhandhil in the Cretan quarter, after acquiring knowledge from the boat builders on Kalymnos. Helping him build boats was Ziya Güvendiren, who is credited with designing and building the first gulet, with a single mast, a mainsail and two jibs.

The gulet developed when fishing became big business, and trawlers and seiners required nets to be towed and pulled on board over the stern without fear of fouling the propellers. They were also used by sponge fishermen to drag the seabed with a *gangava*. This led to the design of a semi-circular transom, cut sharply away beneath the deck. The legacy of this innovation is the capacious, divan-lined aft deck fit for a sultana, while uncluttered deck housing allows sunbathers to be laid end to end. Many gulets do not even possess a set of sails. Usually fitted out with en-suite showers, boats sleep up to twenty, and two or three of the deckhands will spend the season kipping in what is little more than the chain locker at the forward end of the boat.

Built of white, red and black Aegean pine, gulets can take between nine months and two years to complete, costing €75,000 and upwards. Traditionally the timber must be felled during a full moon, when there is less likelihood of worm, and felling is best in the summer months, when the timber is full of sap. Two ceremonies mark the progress of the boat. The first, when the last piece of decking is in place, is celebrated with *baklava*, a kind of 'topping out' when sweetmeats are eaten. The second is the launching ceremony – sometimes no small accomplishment for boats that have to be brought down narrow streets to the shore from inland yards. This being a Muslim country, however, there is no place for a champagne 'christening' and a sheep or cow is traditionally slaughtered instead, its blood smeared on the bow as a blessing, a custom that is probably as old as Homer.

Homer's description of Odysseus building a seaworthy boat in just four days shows that the poet knew more than the rudiments of constructing a traditional vessel. The art of boat building in the Mediterranean and Aegean is deep in the DNA. In Classical times the eastern Mediterranean's major power was Egypt, but the Nile region lacked timber, and papyrus bundled together made insubstantial warships. In the 3rd century BC, when the Carians had already made a name for themselves under their brilliant naval commanders, queens Artemisia I and II, Ptolemy II ordered warships to be built in Bodrum and other parts of the eastern Mediterranean where oak and cyprus grew.

Ptolemy II was the son of Ptolomy I, a general in the army of Alexander the Great that had destroyed Halicarnassus and taken much of the wind out of the shipbuilders' sails. Realising

THE FISHERMAN OF HALICARNASSUS

that his one weakness was a lack of a navy, Alexander had progressed along the coast capturing and destroying ports as he went, so that ships could not be used against him.

Construction and maintenance continued on a small scale, but apart from maintaining the fleet of the Knights of St John, there was no further call for ship building. In 1671 the Turkish traveller Evliya Çelebi passed through Bodrum on his way to Mecca. He described it as *"a small town with poor houses, without mosque, inn, baths or market, surrounded by vineyards and olive groves, which make up the livelihood of the inhabitants".* There were no buildings east of the castle.

In the following century there was a need for ships to repel increasing attacks by local pirates. As luck would have it, the town came under the jurisdiction of Mustafa Pasha of Kızılhisar. This seasoned sailor began wholesale improvements in the town, constructing the Ottoman shipyards whose ruins lie in a tranquil space at the back of Bodrum Marina, approached today through the Tiger Tower. For labour, he attracted boat builders from the islands who became the first modern Greek settlers of the town. He also had built, in 1720, the large mosque, sometimes referred to as the Old Mosque (Eski Cami) on the east side of the harbour, in İskele Square.

The first orders for ships for the Sultan, however, did not arrive until a decade or so after his death, when Turkey found itself at war with Russia. In July 1770, the Ottoman navy under Grand Admiral Mandalzade Hüsameddin was caught napping some 175 kilometres north at Çeşme. Russia's Baltic fleet, unhindered by the West's great powers, had sailed down from St Petersburg and entered the Mediterranean through the Straits of Gibraltar. Trapped in the port, the Ottoman fleet was destroyed largely by fire ships sent among them, and for several years afterwards the Russians were able to sail unopposed around the Aegean.

The Grand Admiral was sacked for his incompetence, to be replaced by Cafer Pasha, who had been one of the commanders at the battle of Çeşme. It fell to him to organise the replenishment of the Ottoman fleet, and he had to look no further than the shipyards in Bodrum that his father had begun. Cafer Pasha also built the large tomb which he shares with his father beneath the shady pines in the old cemetery behind the dockyard where the town's elite lie. Now part of the dockyard gardens, it is an atmospheric, tranquil place.

At the beginning of the 1950s, when the Fisherman's friends were starting to join him on his Blue Voyages, there was no tradition of holiday-making on boats in Bodrum. At that time there were some three hundred fishing boats based around the harbour, according to the travel writer Freya Stark, who came by in 1952 with two companions on a 33-foot London-built motor sailer when researching her book, *The Lycian Shore*. The *Elfin* belonged to the British consul in Izmir and it was, she surmised, the first boat ever to have sailed from Izmir along the Aegean and Mediterranean coasts of Turkey entirely for pleasure.

Now thousands of people are able to enjoy the pleasure of ploughing the coasts' blue waters, of listening to the flap of sails and the murmur of the engines, feeling the gentle heel of the decks and the light rocking through starlit nights, just as the Fisherman of Halicarnassus did, but in much more comfort. He would be the last person to begrudge such luxury, knowing that the visitor would be experiencing his Blue Voyage.

9. BLUE VOYAGE, TURQUOISE COAST, WHITE AND WINE-DARK SEAS

"Here was a sense of profoundness enveloping us in its infinity. The great archipelago, darkening in the turquoise of the evening – the old sea showed me its majestic presence. The seas cracked upon the horizon without warning like a vast blue thundering infinity. It was a deep blue roar... I felt as if I was watching infinity from the hill I was standing on."

This was the Fisherman's first glimpse of the sea at Bodrum, recorded in *Mavi Sürgün* (*The Blue Exile*). Hooked from the start, he began half a century of exploration of its seductive waters. On his arrival in the town he had rushed to the shore, only to be thwarted: the conditions of his exile meant he could not sail on the blue waters that so caught his imagination. In the town's cafés and on the harbour front, he spent many hours listening to fishermen and sponge divers, trying to imagine what their voyages must have been like. During the last half of his sentence, which he served in Constantinople, he dreamed of the blue waters he would soon be sailing, exploring the bays and islands and the forgotten civilisations of the coasts. These would be discoveries he would not want to keep for himself: part of the pleasure would be to share his enthusiasm with his literary friends.

On those early Blue Voyages he would cast off with minimal provisions – cheese and bread, tomatoes, olives, melons and ice, tobacco and raki, just a bottle of which might buy a bed for the night in a fishing village ashore, though the deck or a beach was usually quite adequate for sleeping. For days on end he and his friends would live beyond earshot of radios and out of sight of newspapers. Nothing from the outside world would interfere with their communing with nature and getting back to their roots. It was a time to remember that man connects to the earth, to realise that most of the planet is water, just as most of the human body is water, and that the sea, like blood, tastes of salt. These were the thoughts of Cevat Şakir Kabaağaçlı on his Blue Voyages.

Cevat Şakir was the founder of Blue Voyages but Sabahattin Eyüboğlu was the one to coin the name *Mavi Yolculuk*, according to Azra Erhat. Her book of that name, published in 1962, was dedicated to Sabahattin, who first joined the Fisherman in 1945, and from 1957 organised many Blue Voyages himself. Erhat's book introduced the world to their adventures, explaining what it was like on the cruises, what provisions they took, the sleeping bags and fishing equipment, and the activities they invented and enjoyed. They would make flags to fly, and once turned a bicycle wheel into a windmill. Azra Erhat says that even her closest friends in Istanbul could not understand why they would want to suffer the discomforts and privations of a Blue Voyage, asking, "How can you live in such poverty?"

They were hippies a decade ahead of their time.

Soon the sailing waters began to be popularised in the press. In 1969 *National Geographic* ran a feature titled 'Yankee Sails Turkey's History-Haunted Coast' in a special issue that has become a collectors' item. Its cover story was a full report on Apollo 11 and the first explorers on the moon, with an accompanying vinyl recording on which Neil Armstrong announces the steps he is taking for mankind. The report from Turkey by seasoned sailors Irving and Electa Johnson was of a journey of exploration closer to home. For two decades the couple had been taking pictures and writing stories for the magazine from around the world from a succession of beautiful sailing yachts all called *Yankee*. For this forty-eight-page article, their 50-foot ketch explored the Blue Voyagers' coasts.

Starting at Rhodes, they headed east along the Mediterranean coast, returning the same way, and calling in at Bodrum before heading up the Aegean to Istanbul where they arrived at the same time that another epic adventure was ending. The yachtsman Sadun Boro, later a resident of Bodrum, had at that moment arrived from his round-the-world voyage. Bunting decorated *Kismet*, the first solo circumnavigating Turkish yacht, as she arrived in front of Dolmabahçe Palace, with *Yankee* breezing by a few yards away.

The Blue Voyagers' coast was still virgin, out of sight of international tourism and it had yet to market itself abroad. There is no mention of Blue Voyages in the article, and Irving Johnson dubbed this 'The Pirate Coast' or 'The Sailing Coast'. It had been only seven years since the magazine had been printed in full colour, and the illustrations and photographs have the distinctive quality of their time, making the views look like a lost world. Bodrum then appeared to be a quiet village with no more than a dozen boats in its harbour and no sign of Cevat Şakir.

There is, however, a fine full-page portrait of a laughing man with a grey goatee beard, wearing an indigo shirt, cravat and white woollen hat. The caption reads: *"Expressive hands and face help Suat Şakir Kabaagaç tell a story. The gifted raconteur and notable citizen of the little town of Selimiye often entertains visitors with tales with his store of local lore and history."*

Suat had followed his older brother's example and was living among the fishermen at Side, in Antalya province. He and his wife Mizou had first seen its ancient Greek settlement of Selimiye a few years earlier on a Blue Voyage with Cevat. They became the first people to open a guest house in the village, and they encouraged others to offer rooms to visitors, too, although to begin with many of them refused to take money from their welcome guests. By a Roman arch they ran a restaurant, Pamphylia, that became so well known that Suat is considered to have done for Side what Cevat had done for Bodrum, and in 2010 it was proposed that a statue should be erected to him in recognition of his contribution to tourism in the 'museum city'.

The people of Bodrum were equally reluctant to take paying guests. The idea of taking money from strangers *"was met with bewilderment and even horror,"* according to the writer Fatma Mansur, *"and many of the early tourists stayed in some of the best homes in Bodrum without paying. In 1960 the Tourism Association devised a way to save the hosts from embarrassment: they would get the money from the tourists and give it to the hosts afterwards."* But they soon got the hang of it.

Companionability was all-important for Blue Voyage passengers. In her 2004 memoirs, Hughette Eyüboğlu describes "a sense of blue" when she wrote: *"Experience has taught me that even if you take a trip in the most luxurious of boats, it may very well turn out to be a nightmare if your captain is not a capable and pleasant individual. You must also have the luck of travelling among pleasant people, because the success of the trip is directly related to the amount of 'blue' found in each of the participants."*

Hughette, a Canadian, married Mehmet Eyüboğlu, the son of Sabahattin's brother, the poet and artist Bedri Rahmi. They went on a number of Blue Voyages and Rahmi bought an old Greek house in Bodrum. One twelve-day cruise from Marmaris in 1973 was, Hughette says, "the best Blue Trip of all

73

times". There were card games and cooking lessons, visits to Lycian sites, nights slept beneath stars and an evening dedicated to the colour yellow. Her father-in-law was in excellent form and asked everyone on the boat to find oddly-shaped rocks on which to draw fish or mermaids, or a few lines of his poems, while he drew portraits on shells, sandals, biscuits and the rims of summer hats. Bedri Rahmi always left his mark along the way, painting on stones and rocks where they landed. Behind a fountain in a popular anchorage for Blue Voyagers on the western side of the Gulf of Fethiye, he painted a large, colourful fish that can still be seen in the bay that has been named after him. Sometimes artists were put ashore with their easels and canvases, and at the end of their holiday, says Erhat, they all returned from Blue Voyages inspired by the colours and sights they had seen, and their work was visibly affected.

Cevat Şakir himself wrote: *"If that blue is the sea's own, then dip your pen into it and write blue, blue on sheets of white."* Many of his stories and books contain the words 'Aegean' 'Mediterranean' and 'Sea' in their titles. But one of his best known novels is *Aganta, Burina, Burinata* (1945), which translates as something like 'haul the bowlines in tight'. The more you pulled on the ropes, the faster the boat would travel. It was a metaphor for life.

"One must go aboard a ship which is as small as a nutshell, steal the wind with a tiny piece of canvas with an aspiration of discovering, sailing ahead and progressing. One must ignore others' attempts to prevent one from sailing by reason of dangers of the sea and the possibility of death. One must ignore them, set out and find new places, new worlds."

Fishermen and sailors in *Aganta, Burina, Burinata* shout the words, at the land and at the sea and at the sky, challenging the stars. The shout goes up when they set sail, and when the wind fills their sails. "*Aganta!*" becomes a greeting, a comradely cry. It is as irresistible as the call of the sea itself. The protagonist, working on a passenger ship, is envious of men on a working boat pitting themselves against the elements:

"*I saw a small sailing ship whose deck was completely covered with water. While we were making headway quite easily, she was going through a life-and-death struggle and it was such a glorious struggle. While our passengers were eating almonds and flirting with each other on the upper deck, my fellow sailors were fighting against the sea with the innocence of their bare chests; they were fighting like lions. If only I could have joined them.*"

Yet the Fisherman knew full well the perils of the sea. His short story, 'The Karabulut Family' tells of the last three male generations of a local family, "*once numerous in the area of Bodrum, Marmaris and Küllük*". Grandfather, father and two small children were all in a boat with a cargo of coal. When they were passing between the island of Rhodes and Sümbeki the sky turned to the colour of the coal and a tornado headed towards them. To keep their spirits high in the rising storm they began to sing, and the keeper of the Tekiburnu lighthouse could only look on in despair as "*the tornado tossed the last Karabuluts into the air, together with their songs, their last prayers and the flying sails like pieces of paper burning in the roaring fire, and mixed the lightning with the clouds.*"

A Blue Voyager today, eating almonds and flirting on the aft deck of a gulet, is unlikely to see sailors fighting like lions against a storm. Most of the time the water is calm and astonishingly blue, a sapphire or navy of infinite depth, in metres and in centuries as well as in its shade. This is the 'wine-dark sea' (οίνοπα πόντον) of Homer, a phrase that uncorks its infinite richness. The phrase is used, for example, in the opening chapters of the *Odyssey*. With the goddess Athene at his side, Odysseus's son, Telemachus, sets sail from

Ithaca under the cover of night in search of his father: "*And now, out of the West, Athene with the flashing eyes called up for them a steady following wind and sent it singing over the wine-dark sea.*"

Translating Homer has always been a challenge. The first English version of the *Iliad* was by Arthur Hall, the MP for Grantham, and it was published in 1581. By the time Cevat Şakir was studying history at Oxford, there had been around seventy English translations, most of them towards the end of the 19th century. Among the enthusiastic Classical scholars was the Prime Minister, William Gladstone, who wrote *Studies on Homer and the Homeric Age*, in which a chapter is devoted to Homer's colour descriptions: "*...of light shadow and darkness, he had lively and most poetical perceptions*" but his ideas of colour were "*as yet undigested*". Gladstone concluded that a lack of colour descriptions suggested that ancient Greeks saw colours differently from Victorian Europeans. A year after the book came out, Charles Darwin's *On the Origin of Species* was published, and it wasn't long before speculation began that a sense of colour had to be acquired, that the perception of the early Greeks was far behind "other countries of the east", and would evolve as civilisations evolved.

It started a debate that went on a long time. Homer is not devoid of colour references: "red-haired Menalaus", "the blue-eyed maid", and dawns that are poetically described as crimson and rose-tinted. But it is translation as much as perception that is a problem: *kyanos* (hence cyan), the Greek word for blue, is used by Homer to describe Hector's hair.

The modern world is a highly visual one, enriched with synthetic colours, but in the ancient world only blazing colours such as red or gold seem to have been worthy of note. There are no descriptions of the sea being blue in the earliest texts. The Bible uses the Hebrew word *tehelet* to describe the sea, meaning purple, a colour more like wine. In *Old Calabria* (1915), Norman Douglas wrote of the southern Italians around the Ionian sea: "*Stones are white or black; wine is white or black; prepared olives are white or black…of blue, they have not the faintest conception, probably because there are so few blue solids in nature. Max Müller* [the German philologist] *holds the idea of blue to be quite a modern acquisition on the part of the human race. So a cloudless sky is declared to be 'quite white'. I once asked a lad as to the colour of the sea which, at that moment, was the most brilliant sapphire blue. He pondered a while and then said: 'Pare come fosee un colore morto' – a sort of dead colour.*"

In the end, though, it is simply the poverty of languages that affects colour perception. In his introduction to the enduring Penguin Classic *Odyssey*, which he translated, E.V. Rieu confesses: "*Over the 'wine-dark' sea I have abandoned my own principles and thrown up my pen in despair. I know that it is wrong and ought to be 'wine-faced' or something to that effect. But the English language has failed me, just as it fails me, though for other reasons, when I am tempted to write of the 'fishy' sea.*"

In her translation of Homer into modern Turkish, Azra Erhat called the wine-dark sea *menekse rengi deniz*, meaning a violet-coloured sea, which is much easier to imagine. *Menekse* is used for both the colour and the flower, the African violet.

The Turkish call the Mediterranean Sea *Akdeniz*, the White Sea. This is Anatolia's southern shore. Its northern shore is on the Black Sea, *Karadeniz*, following Asian traditions in which seas were once given colours according to their points of the compass: black for north, yellow for east, red for south, white for east. Blue is also used for south, though the word in Turkish, *gök*, can also mean sky. *Ova* means plain, so the Gulf of Gökova on which Bodrum lies is a southerly, sky-blue plain.

Each sea has its own peculiarities, tides, salinity and plankton that causes it to be clear or cloudy, green, grey, brown or blue. An abundance of Mediterranean sea grass around the coast helps oxygenate the water and keep it clear. It depends on the colour of the sky, too.

In *The Sea of Islands: The Mediterranean*, the Fisherman described the sight of teaming shoals of sardines at night in the waters around Bodrum, and their significance in the White Sea.

"*From the twilight of the depths a fateful life struggle had surfaced. The vast bosom of the waters did not seem large enough to take in this life flood. The depths became an abyss of life and death. These fish are the chief birth givers of the Mediterranean. Togetherness is their life-law. They live together, love and rejoice together, and they die together. The herd is like one fish. In this world of fish that knows no separation and reunion, making love is a swimming adventure. In the course of their swimming they produce eggs, milk and a flood of offspring. The waves of the sea become sticky, and the water elastic. Within this life-yeast, life itself boils. Their eggs are a tiny round blue lantern in the vast darkness of the sea. This discharged volcano of egg and milk stifles the sea whose ability to choke is well known. At night miles and miles of sea turn milky white with these currents of fish and motherhood. The sea like Divine Light! This is the reason why the sea is called the White Sea in Turkish.*"

As for the Turquoise Coast, the name is given to the Mediterranean coast from Marmaris eastwards. It takes its name from the colourful water found at places such as Ölüdeniz, an idyllic beach where the water is startlingly turquoise. *Ölü deniz* translates as the Dead Sea, though in English the lagoon is often called the Blue Sea. 'Dead' here does not mean *colore morto*, but the fact that the waters are invariably calm.

Weather is tempered by the mountainous landscape. The land around the Gulf of Gökova rises to 1,000 metres, while the Taurus Mountains along the Lycian coast are three times as high, their snowcapped peaks incongruously peering into warm blue skies. These mountains and their deep valleys block and funnel winds to keep sailors on their toes. But what ruffles the sea most is the *meltem*, the north wind that appears in summer when the air rises in the landmass to the east as it heats, and air rushes in from the cooler northwest to take its place. It blows from mid-June to mid-September and is at its worst in July and August. Beginning in the morning, it builds through the day, sometimes lasting several days. For windsurfers, of course, this is a blessing, and they head for Fener and other beaches on the extreme southwest corner of the Bodrum peninsula, where winds can reach Beaufort force 7.

Francis Beaufort, deviser of the wind scale named after him, was a British naval officer and cartographer, and in 1812 he sailed down from Smyrna to 'Boodroom' to begin a season of mapping the entire coast, which until then had never been properly charted. The results were published in *Karamania, or a Brief Description of the South Coast of Asia-Minor and of the Remains of Antiquity*. Beaufort was astounded at the quantity of Classical material he saw along the coast, much of which, as Cevat Şakir and his friends later found, was only revealed when viewed from the sea. Beaufort wrote extensive descriptions of the geology, topography and antiquities, and detailed the progress of his voyage, but at no point does he mention the colour of the sea.

Whatever hue of blueness, whatever tone the sky, the water around these coasts is almost invariably crystal clear. With no tides to churn up the seabed, and little plankton, the water can be so transparent that a swimmer will hang on to the side of a boat for fear of falling. Painted combers or rainbow wrasse flit by like birds in an empty sky, ignorant of the colour

79

of the water they are swimming in, be it blue or white or turquoise. But for the Fisherman of Halicarnassus, Bodrum, the Aegean, the Mediterranean all seemed an eternal blue.

"The sea and the sky cannot be more blue than they are in Bodrum," he wrote. *"Blue explodes, absolute, deafening, infinite."*

10. GREEKS

Cevat Şakir might not have known Devlet Hanım, but he would certainly have known her story. When he arrived in Bodrum, she was in her thirties and could be seen around town like many other women, dressed in black with a traditional black-and-white striped shawl covering her head. The shawl also covered the scars where once her ears had been. They had been hacked off sixteen years earlier when she was a young girl in Crete. During a night of savage slaughter in the Cretans' struggle for independence from Ottoman rule, she was presumed dead among what some claimed to be 3,000 dispatched Turks. Her ears had been sliced off simply to take her gold earrings.

This is one of thousands of horrific tales that were told on both sides throughout the region as the Ottoman Empire fell apart. The conflict destroyed friendships and neighbourhoods and created divisions as deep as any between nations. The final outcome was draconian. Communities and whole towns were uprooted as populations were exchanged. In the course of just a few years 1,300,000 Orthodox Christians from Turkey arrived in Greece, creating a massive refugee problem that resulted in hundreds of new villages, while Athens, which had been little more than a village a century earlier, had to throw up thousands of homes. From Christian Greece came around 390,000 Muslims, most unable to speak Turkish, to move into the houses the 'Greeks' had left behind.

With the expulsion went much of Turkey's commercial life, and though the measure did not apply in the islands of the Dodecanese that surround Bodrum, as they were then still under Italian occupation, the Aegean and Mediterranean coasts where seafaring Greeks had predominated became eerily quiet. Many whitewashed stone houses, architecturally distinct and similar to Greek island buildings, were simply abandoned to die back into the land from which they had been hewn. Their remoteness and problems with land registration were often hinderances to their re-occupation.

For most of the 20th century, Kalkan and Kaş in Lycia, attractive fishing villages familiar to Blue Voyagers, were all but deserted, as were houses around the castle in the old town of Marmaris. Near Fethiye, the 6,000 inhabitants of Levissi were packed off to Athens and 2,000 buildings were left to fall into ruin. Renamed Kayaköy (Stone Village), it remains a ghost town, inspiring Louis de Bernière's novel, *Bird Without Wings*.

The population exchange occurred at the end of the War of Independence, in 1923, the year that the Republic was declared and two years before Cevat Şakir set foot in Bodrum. By the time he arrived, the exchanged Muslims, mostly from Crete, had settled into the empty houses in the town's Greek quarter along Kumbahçe beach to the east of the castle, joining the earlier refugees from the Greco–Turkish war, and bringing their seafaring ways. These typical Greek houses, flat-roofed two-storey white boxes, give Bodrum its character, and planning laws guarantee the style is preserved. It was in one of these waterside buildings, now a restaurant opposite the Atatürk elementary school, that Cevat Şakir first lived.

After more than 2,000 years, since Ionian and Dorians had first settled among the Carians, Lycians and other peoples of Anatolia, the Greeks' story had, theoretically, come to an end. Yet the terms Greek and Turk, Christian and Muslim, make harsh divisions among peoples that are as mixed as any Macedonian salad. Population transfers had been a feature of the first centuries of Ottoman rule, and until the early 19th-century, reforms communities of Christians, Jews and Muslims had lived alongside each other in a system of *millets* (literally 'nations') in which they dispensed their own confessional laws (Cannon, Halakhah and Sharia), though non-Muslims paid higher taxes, making an incentive to convert. Within this diversity, Greeks spoke their own language and in Crete even learned to write it in the Arabic letters of the Turks, while Karamanlides were Orthodox Greeks from eastern Anatolia who spoke Turkish but wrote it in Greek letters. Yet it was still a Muslim state, and until the system ended in the early 19th century Christian children, mainly from the Slavic Balkans, had by custom been sent to Constantinople to be trained for the Sultan's standing army of Janissaries. This was considered a good career for a village lad – or a cruel imposition, depending on the historic view. Frequently rebelling, they were finally banned and military schools were introduced. In a country with little educational provision these became the backbone of the educated middle class.

The break-up of the empire caused populations to re-imagine their identities, and for this they looked to their roots. As communities tried to work out which 'nation' they belonged to, the choice became governed by their place of worship rather than either their place of birth, their length of ancestral residence or their first language. Religion was a defining factor, and in this, outside Catholic, Protestant and Orthodox forces exerted their influence where they could.

Greece regained its independence in 1832. Although it had not been a nation since pagan Athens became a Roman province in 146BC, it could lay claim to being a core part of the Byzantine Empire. In AD330 Constantine, the first Roman

Emperor to convert, established Christianity in the ancient Greek city of Byzantios, Roman Byzantium, on the Bosphoros, changing its name to Constantinople. After the fall of Rome, the Eastern Church broke from the West, gradually transforming into the Byzantine Empire, in which Greek, the language of the New Testament, was spoken. For 2,000 years it was the church more than anything else that had kept a Greek identity and idea of nationhood alive. The primate of the Greek Orthodox Church today remains in Istanbul.

When Constantinople fell to the Ottoman Turks in 1453, the mantle of the Orthodox church was passed to Moscow, which described itself as the 'third Rome.' Today, Russian emporia dominate the centre of Demre (former Myra), a Blue Voyage port of call on the Lycian coast. This was the birthplace of St Nicholas, Russia's patron saint, otherwise celebrated as Father Christmas, whose red-coated statue looks incongruous in the Mediterranean sun. Meanwhile, the two-headed eagle of Byzantium was taken up by the Romanov Russian imperial house and today the symbol flies on the flags of the Greek Orthodox Church at Easter and on other special occasions.

Cevat Şakir's mother was Cretan and he was born on the island in 1890 when his father was serving as a local governor. It was an Ottoman possession then, and had been since the 17th century. Janissaries and bureaucrats had settled on the island and intermarried. When the Greek War of Independence began in 1821, Greeks on the island initiated a series of insurrections against the Turkish authorities, assuming all Muslims – about forty percent of the islanders – to be non-Greek. There were outbursts on either side, and these continued up until 1897 when the mainland Greeks, who by then had gained their independence, sent a force to try to capture the island, sparking the Greco–Turkish War in which little Devlet Hanım had her ears chopped off.

As one war followed another, and independence movements rose up against the empire, refugee Muslims began to arrive in their many thousands, from Armenia and the Caucasus in the east to the Balkans in the west. A million Muslim Turks, whose families had been living in the Balkans for five centuries, found themselves as refugees in their own, strange lands. Most were forced to walk all the way. Territory was disappearing fast. In the Turco–Italian War of 1911–12, the Dodecanese, the islands around Bodrum, were lost to the Italians along with Libya. In the Balkan Wars of 1912–13, the Ottomans were stripped of all their remaining European possessions bar a slither of Thrace west of Istanbul, the three percent of Turkey that remains in Europe.

With few resources, Greece was neutral at the start of the First World War but with Turkey joining the Central Powers (Germany, Austria-Hungary and Bulgaria), it was soon sucked into the side of the Allies who saw its strategic position as vital. Greeks in Turkey were thereafter treated with suspicion, and when ships from the French and British navies took shots at Bodrum castle, able-bodied male Christians in the town were sent to Central Anatolia for the duration of hostilities. It was the last they saw of Bodrum: after the war they were dispatched directly to Greece.

Defeat in the First World War left the whole country open to take-over by the Allied powers. Even before hostilities ended, Britain, France and Italy were jostling for pieces of the cake. And when the Italians landed in Antalya and began heading north and around the coast towards Smyrna, the Council of Four (including the USA) approved Greece's occupation of Aegean Turkey.

On May 15, 1919 the first of a force of 20,000 Greeks landed in Smyrna, a city of roughly equal numbers of Christians and Muslims, as well as lesser numbers of

Armenians and Jews. But they did not stop there. This was their golden moment, a chance to realise the dream of a *Magáli Idéa*, a 'Greater Greece' and a new Byzantium that would reclaim not only the Mediterranean and Aegean seaboards but also the Black Sea region, where Jason and the Argonauts had sailed and which had been settled by Pontic Greeks. With the backing of the Allied powers, the Greek forces advanced on Anatolia.

The Turkish government was outraged and the people rallied to resist the invaders. On March 19, 1920, British troops in Constantinople entered and forcibly disbanded parliament, sending a number of MPs into exile in Malta. Ten months earlier, on the day Greek forces landed in Smyrna, Mustafa Kemal, hero of Gallipoli, had been sent from Constantinople to Samsun on the Black Sea. Though this was an official mission to seek out unrest, he had been fostering plans for a national resistance, and when he was recalled to Constantinople, he resigned from the army, which brought him a death sentence. Mustafa Kemal's 'inspection' unit from Samsun formed the core of the National Delegation that eventually set up a new capital far from the gunboats and the sea in Ankara, then called Angora, a small town best known for the mohair from its goats and the wool from its rabbits. There, on April 23, 1920, he convened the first Grand National Assembly, today celebrated in Turkey as Children's Day.

In Constantinople, Sultan Mehmet VI was politically impotent, and in August he was handed a humiliating treaty to sign by the Allied powers. He acquiesced. The Treaty of Sèvre left the northwest, plus Constantinople, under the control of the Tripartate powers (the US did not want to be part of it). The southeast was to remain under the French sphere of influence, and the southwest was to become the Italian colony of Lycia. This included Bodrum, where Italian troops were garrisoned in the castle, and the neighbouring province of Antalya.

The first shots in the War of Independence had been fired against the French in the southeast the previous December, and when Greek forces landed, Turks flooded to their country's defence. Among them were the nomadic Yörük population around the Aegean who joined guerilla bands of armed irregulars from the ranks of Zeybeks, the traditional protectors of local communities led by chieftains called 'Efe's.

Seeing the strength of the re-born nation, the French and Italians soon withdrew, but the British remained committed to supporting Greece and their cause of a *Magáli Idéa*, though their greater interest was in gaining a firm ally in the Eastern Mediterranean. The campaign proved an unmitigated disaster. Greeks still resident in Anatolia were now seen as potential enemies of Turkey, even if their families had lived in the country since the time of Herodotus and no longer spoke the Greek language.

After more than three years of fighting, the Greek army was driven back to the sea at Smyrna where it mingled with the civilian population and fleeing Christians, both Greek and Armenian. A crush of people overwhelmed the dockside awaiting rescue. The town was set alight. Evacuation by ship was slow. Thousands died as the 'Pearl of the Aegean' the most cosmopolitan city in Anatolia and Turkey's second largest port after Istanbul, the town where Cevat Şakir would spend the last twenty-five years of his life, burned for more than a week.

"The waters of Smyrna were choked with dead bodies," Lawrence Durrell later wrote. *"But it is more than the injustice, cruelty, the madness of the episode that sticks in the mind of the modern Greek. It is also a loss of the richness, a lost peace of mind. If he is in exile, he returns again and again in his dreams."*

The Turks had dreams, too, of a country they could call

their own. When the Turkish army turned north towards Constantinople and Thrace, Britain, deserted by her European allies, called on the Commonwealth for support: only New Zealand responded positively, but troops were never sent. It was recognised that the Turks had won the day. Constantinople was regained, and the Treaty of Sèvre was never ratified. It would not be mentioned again except as a byword in Turkey for infamy.

The Greek invasion of Turkey and its repulsion were seen as the final straw in the conflict between the two neighbours. Plans to exchange populations that had been mooted as early as 1914, when both the Greek and Turkish governments were in favour, were now agreed as part of the 1923 Treaty of Lausanne, though by this time nearly a million of the 1,300,000 exiled Greeks had already fled. The treaty was the final reckoning of the war, defining the Turkish Republic's boundaries and enacted two years before the Fisherman first set eyes on Bodrum.

By the time he arrived, conflict had exhausted the country, and many people were trying to put their lives back together. In remote Bodrum, Cevat Şakir was far removed from his family roots, his past, and he could start afresh. Here were people who knew nothing of his hopes or his heritage, and he could live among them unencumbered. Nor was he a part of the changes the town had seen during the past tumultuous two decades. Dropped out of the blue into Bodrum, he could appreciate things just as he found them, including the maritime culture of the Muslim Greeks, and from their number he would find his third wife. He appreciated their culinary taste, too, which included bloodless seafood such as shrimps and octopus, which devout Muslims did not eat.

A shepherd from Crete, Ali Subaşı, who became a ship's cook after arriving in Bodrum, is credited with opening the first restaurant in the town in 1927. Beside the harbour promenade near the yacht club, Körfez (Gulf) remains in the same family's hands, and grilled shrimp and octopus are still on the menu. Cevat Şakir was a regular. According to Ali's son, Hassan, the Fisherman used to mimic a Greek accent to ask the patron, "What have you got today, Subaşı?" Other recognisable diners have included the effeminate Zeki Müren, the popular composer of Makam, Turkish traditional music. Müren was Bodrum's best-known celebrity resident, an unexpected cultural icon in a patriarchal country, and his house here was turned into a museum after his death, on stage, in 1996.

A number of Turkish presidents have dined in Körfez, but Atatürk never visited Bodrum, though his legacy is still keenly felt. Turkish people remain grateful to him for preventing their country from being wiped off the map, and his statues crop up throughout the country, in private gardens as well as in public spaces. Museums have been made in houses where he set foot, and he is particularly in evidence on October 29, Republic Day.

The Turks' successes ended, however, at the sea shore, where all they could do was stop and stare out at the islands lost forever from their grasp. Deprived of a navy, which had been commandeered by the Allies, the Turkish military power extended only as far as the water's edge. A political barrier was now drawn between the islands and the continent to which they geologically and historically belonged.

Territorial waters were extended to three miles under the Lausanne Treaty and later increased to six miles. (Further friction was caused in the 1990s when the Greeks attempted to increase their territorial waters to the EU norm of twelve miles.) The three-mile limit meant that islands close to shore were safe, and these included all the islands in the Gulf of Gökova. But even today, a boat heading directly across the

Gulf from Bodrum to Knidos must swerve to the east to avoid the Greek territorial waters that ripple into the mouth of the Gulf from the island of Kos. On headlands and above villages all around the coast, Blue Voyagers will see the Turkish flag flying, as if the territory had only just been won. Greeks fly their flags too, so there can be no doubt whose country a mariner is setting foot on.

Tensions between the two communities across this imaginary line come and go. Conflicts occur over territorial disputes, such as the Greek military coup and subsequent Turkish invasion of Cyprus in 1974. Sometimes it doesn't take much – a perceived insult, an unpopular football result – to get the blood rising again, to bring to the surface the old tales, like that of Devlet Hanım, or the horrendous murder of Chrysostomos, Bishop of Smyrna, by the Turkish mob.

But politicians long ago realised it was time to move on. Diplomatic relations between the two countries were established in 1925 and in 1934 Eleftheros Venizelos, Greek prime minister and architect of the Smyrna landing, put forward Mustafa Kemal Atatürk as a contender for the Nobel Peace Prize. The two sides came together in the Second World War, too. In 1941, after the Germans had overrun Greece, the Greek people were starving but the British refused to allow humanitarian aid to pass through their sea blockade. In the end, ignoring the blockade, relief ships organised by the Turkish Red Crescent at the request of Turkey's neutral government and with a large response from the Turkish people, were sent from Istanbul, with agreement from the Germans. The Turkish ambassador in London simply told the British government that the shipments were going ahead. The ships got through, and when more followed, Britain relented.

Kos is well within view of Bodrum, but during the Fisherman's time there was little or no trade between Anatolia and the Greek islands. An exception was the workers from the barren island of Patmos who visited the Meander Valley (Büyük Menderes Vadisi) to harvest fertile lands bequeathed to the island's 11th-century monastery of St John by the Byzantine emperor. This annual event apparently continued with impunity during the Ottoman era. Otherwise links were rare, as Lord Kinross discovered after spending several seasons travelling the length of the Anatolian coast for his 1956 book *Europa Minor*, much of it on board the *Elfin*, the motor vessel belonging to the British Consul General in Izmir in which Freya Stark had sailed.

"Only in Bodrum," he wrote, *"did we find a disposition even to fraternise: a boat went across almost daily to Kos, and the Turkish harbour master looked forward to a day when intercourse with his Greek neighbours would be freer."*

Today relations are a good deal freer. Ferries run regularly between Bodrum and the Greek islands of Kos, Kalymnos, Nisos, Symi and Rhodes. Day trippers go to meet friends, though passports are needed, and while Turkish passengers must queue at passport control, EU passport holders whistle through. Blue Voyage captains are careful to keep their paperwork in order, and to fly a courtesy Greek flag as they report to the authorities on arrival. But when, in 2012, the five-day Bodrum Cup took in the Greek islands of Kalymnos and Kos for the first time, the feasting, dancing and exchanging of gifts made it seem as if the two communities had never been less than the best of friends.

11. BLUE ANATOLIAN HUMANISM

In 2012, after three years' research, linguists in New Zealand concluded that English is descended from a language that emerged in Anatolia 9,500 years ago. In fact they traced the origin of all Indo-European languages, including Russian, Polish, Persian, Hindi and ancient Greek to Anatolia. Four years earlier, an international study of DNA evidence showed that the Neolithic populations of central and northern Greece, as well as the Minoans in Crete, had arrived from Anatolia around 7,000BC. A year later DNA tests carried out by Turin University concluded that the Etruscii, antecedents of the people of Tuscany and Umbria, also came from Anatolia, from the region around Izmir.

These snippets of news would have delighted Cevat Şakir Kabaağaçlı. They would have been further proof of his conviction that Western civilisation sprang from Anatolia. This was the essential tenet of Blue Anatolian Humanism, the philosophy that developed during days and nights of discussion among the Fisherman and his 'Blue-ist' (*Maviciler*) friends on their voyages along the Caraian and Lycian shores.

For more than a century Turkey had been fishing for a cultural identity, and never had the need to find one been so pressing. The Ottoman Empire into which the Fisherman had been born had been vast. Sofia, Belgrade, Salonika, Damascus, Beirut, Palestine, Alexandria and Cairo were world cities, and many important institutions had been set up in its European territories of Bulgaria and the Balkans. Now these were all gone. Even Constantinople, the Sublime Port of sultans, the city that straddled both Europe and Asia, with a cornucopian history going back more than 1,600 years, could no longer be looked to as the capital. In his first novel, *Aganta, Burina, Burinata*, the Fisherman of Halicarnassus depicts it as a decadent, loveless place, somewhere for sailors to go to find prostitutes.

The brave new Republic established under Mustafa Kemal in 1923 had thrown off the veil of the Ottoman Empire, denying much of the country's past. This meant coming to terms with a new, core identity that was secular and definitely Turkish. It was a dramatic move, but the debate had been going on since the early 19th century, as politicians and intellectuals struggled to imagine a future in which both Arab-Persian and Greco-Roman cultures, East and West, could co-exist. Although Mediterranean peoples share many qualities, it was a dilemma that had been around from the time of Herodotus, and for all the dramatic sweep of Atatürk's wholesale Westernising programme, it remains unresolved to this day.

To break this deadlock, a religiously neutral humanism seemed to be the way forward. Humanism has it roots in the Renaissance, with the rediscovery in Italy of the philosophies and culture of the Greco-Roman world. This infected learning just as much as it did art, and the 13th-century Italian writers Dante and Petrarch are looked on as humanism's founding fathers. The church then was rich and corrupt, and the humanists began to look at the world beyond its reach, studying nature and embarking on scientific enquiry. This did not mean that they were atheists, but humanism was holistic, putting man at the centre of his universe rather than a deity, and holding people responsible for their own actions. Essential to this was the teaching of Latin and Greek, of writers such as Aristotle and Plato, and teachers were hired from Byzantium for the task, particularly after 1453, when many Greek-speaking scholars fled Constantinople after it fell to the Ottoman Turks.

Atatürk's secular, liberal one-party state was essentially humanist and it brought in many dramatic social changes. Western Sunday replaced Eastern Friday as the day of rest, and the Western calendar was adopted. The government-appointed Diyanet, or Presidency of Religious Affairs, replaced the Caliphate, and religious clothing was banned in public. *Medreses*, schools attached to mosques, were closed. Even Robert College had to give up the church-going that had so infuriated young Cevat.

Rules for religious clothing included hats. The crimson flowerpot fez was banned. Introducing his Hat Law of 1925, Mustafa Kemal wore a white cotton Panama, which he favoured in summer. He was otherwise seen in a shiny silk topper or his army regulation Astrakan *kalpak*, a brimless, high hat of lamb's wool. This was not the first hat moment in Ottoman history. The tarboosh, or fez, that Atatürk abolished had arrived in the modernising Tanzimat reforms of 1839, which in their turn had abolished the turban or Turkish knot. The conical scarlet hat, with a tassel, took its name from the Moroccan city of Fes and was worn throughout the Muslim world. Its advantage was that it had no brim, and so touching the forehead to the ground when praying did not require its removal. Without the fez, many ordinary men reached for the cloth or linen cap, which for prayer could simply be reversed – American baseball jocks were not the first to see the advantages of wearing their caps back to front. The Fisherman favoured a black beret, the headgear of the southern European working man, which became his trademark.

Every citizen was now required to use a family name, a

custom not practised by Ottoman Muslims, many of whom had similar names but had simply attached titles – *pasha*, *bey*, *efendi*, *hanim* – or been attributed nicknames to describe careers, characteristics or even personal appearances – Koca (Huge), Kulaksız (Earless) and Kemal, meaning wise or mature, which had been given to Mustafa by his maths teacher: 'Atatürk' was later bestowed by the nation.

Place names with Greek connections would have to change: Smyrna became Izmir, and Constantinople, a name that evoked the first Christian emperor and in Ottoman times had gone under various names, such as Dersaadet and Asitane as well as Konstantinniye, became Istanbul.

The written language changed overnight from one employing Arabic script, used by the elite, to one with a Western, Latin script, based on *kaba Türkçe*, the 'raw Turkish' spoken by the greater populace, which had fewer Arabic and Persian loan words. From now on, only scholars would be able to access the Ottoman past.

There was guaranteed equality for women and a commitment to full education, despite limited funds. Science was high on the agenda, and archaeology was given the serious attention it had lacked under the Ottoman Empire; the first generation of Turkish archaeologists – Arif Müfit Mansel, Ekrem Akurgal and Halet Çambel – began their work. Bright young men were sent to Germany and elsewhere to complete their education, and when Jewish professors began to be ousted from their top-class posts in Germany, they were welcome here.

Still, for some, this was not enough. Modernisation was one thing, but it did not always take away insecurity about a cultural identity. Extreme nationalists continued to search for lines of pure descent into the glory of the past and at the First Turkish History Congress in 1932, when the concept of a particular 'Turkish Humanism' was introduced into the political debate, it was even proposed that "the original of everything in the universe comes from Turkey and that Turks are the most superior race in the world".

Racial superiority was not Atatürk's idea for the Turks, nor would it be the Blue-ists' who believed that the Anatolian character was more than simply DNA. Atatürk died in 1938, on the eve of the Second World War, in which Turkey would remain neutral. His successor was İsmet İnönü, who had been his right-hand man during the War of Independence, and he carried on the Republic's reforms, bringing Turkish humanism to the forefront of government polices. Central to these policies was the Minister for Education, Hasan Ali Yücel, who introduced three key elements: a Translation Office, Village Institutes and the teaching of Greek and Latin in schools.

In spite of the Republic's best intentions, illiteracy in the country was high, and most people in Bodrum would not have been able to read the Fisherman's stories. Eighty-five percent of the population lived in villages, and only seventeen percent of men were literate, 4.2 percent of woman. No more than one in five school-age children were in education. To combat this, Village Institutes, aimed at creating an Anatolian Enlightenment, were set up in places where there had been no education before. Young teachers were trained and sent to help run these Institutes and advise on modern medicines and agricultural methods, as well as giving classroom instruction, which would include music lessons and folk songs.

Among the teachers was Sabahattin Eyüboğlu, whose father had been a member of Atatürk's parliament. He saw the Institutes as being fully committed to the Republic's educational principles, replacing religious morals with work and science ethics. Eyüboğlu was also associate director of The Translation Office, established in 1940. Apart from Aristotle, few Ancient Greek writers had been translated into

Turkish. Over the next few years a total of 1,247 books in modern Turkish were published by the Translation Office, but only thirty-nine were from the East or the Islamic world. Shakespeare, Montaigne and Kafka were among the Western writers Eyüboğlu chose as part of the core curriculum. (Cevat Şakir translated George Bernard Shaw, one of his favouite writers.) Later, Eyüboğlu would defend himself against charges of opening the door to cultural imperialism, saying that Western culture had been nurtured by ancient civilisations and was therefore the property of every nation.

An interest in the Classical world, so important to humanism, sent Eyüboğlu looking for evidence of Greek culture in Anatolia, and in 1945 he went on his first Blue Voyage with Cevat Şakir Kabaağaçlı. In the Fisherman, who was some eighteen years his senior, he found an inspiration, somebody who largely shared his views, with a great depth of knowledge of Anatolian antiquity, who could take him to sites he would later film to help educate the Turkish people about their past.

The second key figure who would develop the philosophy of Blue Anatolian Humanism was a pupil of Eyüboğlu, Azra Erhat, who also worked in the Translation Office. Her sojourns with the Fisherman helped to put Bodrum on the map with her books, *Mavi Anadolu* (*Blue Anatolia*, 1960) and *Mavi Yolculuk* (*Blue Cruise*, 1962). Most importantly she translated Classical Greek texts, including Homer, which she believed would nourish the new Turkish culture as they had nourished the West.

"*Homer is still the most reliable reference for describing and understanding these lands,*" Erhat wrote, "*because he collected what it was in the memories and souls of the local people before written history. That is why his works are immortal.*"

In *The Sixth Continent*, Cevat Şakir writes of the Ionians,

97

the first Greeks in Anatolia: *"They were free of moral gods binding their minds with sacred commands. They were free of the incubus of mythological terrors and hopes of extending into the hereafter. They were free also of the obligation of supporting the vested interests of kings and priests. The human mind was free – it is worth repeating, for the first time in history – to take creation as the Here and Now, and attempt to arrive at a purely naturalistic interpretation of the cosmos."*

This set the Ionians culturally at odds with Athenian Greeks, whom the Fisherman blamed for destroying such freedom of thought. In particular, he pointed to Plato as the perpetrator of this destruction. The Athenian philosopher had brought misery upon the world by his 'dualism', the philosophy that separated the soul from the body, which led to the creation of Western religions. Such philosophy ignored the unity of man, the ideal that was embodied in the work of Homer and the natural philosophy of the atomists. This is how he expressed it in a hand-written note in English exhibited in Bodrum Maritime Museum:

"In Homer ideas follow one another in an unbroken stream rather than being fitted – as in Greece – into a prearranged pattern – sequence rather than antithesis is a peculiarity as much as his whole composition or as his individual cadence. It is the art that conceals art. The skill with which the reader is led so naturally from one to another and the immense range of topics embraced by his work."

In *The Sixth Continent*, Cevat Şakir berates the West for always looking towards Athens and the Greek mainland as the starting point of Western culture, when the focus should be on Anatolia. He points to the small patches of trees from the Miocene period to be found in Bodrum's Muğla Province and elsewhere, which suggest that humans could have survived the last Ice Age here. Anatolians, he explains, then went on to populate Crete and the Cycladic islands where the Minoan cultures flourished from the 27th to the 15th centuries BC. In later centuries Aeolians, Ionians and Dorians were merely returning to the Anatolian shore.

But civilisations are made of many peoples. The Hittites, who came from the east, provided a bridge between the ancient civilisations of Mesopotamia and the Aegean, controlling Anatolia from around 2000 to 1200BC. Their royal library in Hattusas in central Anatolia had tablets written in eight languages.

"*The Hittites came to Asia Minor as barbarians,*" Cevat Şakir wrote. "*They found in the peninsula a civilisation by which they were assimilated.*"

By the time of Athens' ascendency, Anatolian communities were, he believed, far more liberal and advanced. Here drainage and running water was installed while Athens had none, town planning was pioneered, slavery was not developed, and natural philosophy flourished. But in Athens any philosophers who were not in thrall to the gods could expect to be punished – here he might have been thinking of his own punishment at Robert College. As the Fisherman's argument reached its conclusion, his voice would be raised, his arm sweeping wide before coming down with some force on a café table: "*The contempt the philosophers of Athens felt for science arrested human progress for at least 1,000 years!*"

The inhabitants of Anatolia after the Greeks – the Romans and Byzantines, the Crusaders, Venetians, Genoans, Monguls, the Seljuk and Ottoman Turks, not to mention the earlier Carians, Lelegians, Phrygians, and Phoenecians – were all part of the make-up of the modern Anatolian, and they had to be taken into account. Cevat Şakir did not ignore or outcast them. He was proud of the Cretan blood inherited from his mother, just as he could look to the sound Turkish stock of his father. For a brief while after his release from prison in 1921 he even taught in a Sufi tekke in Constantinople and embarked on a translation into English of the works of the Dervish poet Rumi. Figurines of three whirling Dervishes had a permanent place on the writing desk in the house he bought in Gümbet on the west side of Bodrum. However, the downplaying of the Byzantine and Ottoman empires and the emphasis on ancient Greece created a void, a silence of centuries, much as visitors to this coast find today: there are ancient remains and modern houses with little visible in between.

Combined with this fixation on ancient history was a belief in landscape and nature, and how these could and should define a people. The people of Bodrum and the province of Muğla are regarded as having a rough dialect, and Cevat Şakir was convinced that landscape had as much influence on the way that Turkish is spoken as the taught linguistic history, and that the languages of everyone who had ever lived here could be heard in the music of their speech. It was the mountains, the sea, the climate, the vegetation, the diet, the degree of isolation that would shape values, outlooks and beliefs as well as their diction. Here he could point to another ancient local source: Hippocrates of Kos, father of medicine and the idea of 'geographical determinism', the theory that environment influences the temper of nations.

Blue Anatolian Humanism was a pacifist ideology, and Halikarnas Balıkçısı, the Fisherman of Halicarnassus, had many ideas in common with the new Republic but he was also by nature a satirist who would never be in thrall to the establishment. He wrote tales such as 'The Resurrection of the Unknown Soldier', in which the soldier of the title – in fact a trapped underground labourer – makes a ghostly appearance during the Great Wreath-Laying Ceremony on Mount Glory in the fantasy land of Gensiana. Among the potentates and grandees in attendance is the British envoy, *"Lord Swig of Swig, Earl of Workworthy, officer of the order of the Carter* [sic] *in his red coat...shaven all red like a tomato."*

Closer to home, in *Aganta, Burina, Burinata*, he made fun of Village Institutes, though he undoubtedly supported Sabahattin Eyüboğlu's work. In the 1946 novel, earnest young teachers show local peasants how to make use of a thermometer to test the temperature of the soil, to decide the best time for planting. After they have gone, the villagers just laugh and return to their old ways – of dropping their trousers and assessing the earth's temperature with their bare bums.

Although concerned with social issues and supportive of the liberal Republic's reforms, the group by and large had a hands-off approach to political activity. In fact some critics have accused them of not understanding humanism at all, but of simply showing an affection for humans and an enthusiasm for life. They were nevertheless often treated with suspicion by the authorities.

Turkey was on the border with the Soviet Union and a key Nato member, and at times of heightened East–West tension houses of radicals and dissenters were liable to be raided. In 1948 Azra Erhat had been dismissed from Ankara University, accused of harbouring communist sympathies, and spent four months in prison. In 1946 Yücel, the Public Education Minister, who was a philosopher and a Sufi poet, resigned amid accusations that the Village Institutes were "promting communism", and a few years later they were all closed down. In 1960 Sabahattin Eyüboğlu lost his post at Istanbul University in the wake of a military coup, and following a second coup in 1971 he and his wife Magdi were arrested for supposedly starting a communist organisation. Jailed for eight months, he was released without charge.

In Izmir, Cevat Şakir would be harassed by the authorities,

too. His writing was often censored or confiscated and destroyed during raids on his home. But he was not a man to be easily discouraged, and he often saw his surveillance as a game. A cousin recalls an evening out with Cevat who devised a novel way of hitching a lift home. Spotting plainclothes policemen following him, he suggested they pretended to be drunk and lie on the ground, which they did, so the police felt obliged to carry them back to his flat.

In 1961 his outspokenness ended in a third jail term. He was heard loudly arguing in a bar that the crescent moon and star on the flag of the Turkish Republic had nothing to do with Islam or any popular legends, but was a symbol in use since antiquity, and could be seen on monuments throughout Anatolia. As a result he was arrested for insulting the flag, and imprisoned for nine months before being released without charge. Nearly a decade later, when the main street in Bodrum was named after him, he remarked that donkeys and camels would now do to him what the government had done to him all his life.

Such remarks would endear him to the ordinary Turk. His years in jail and his time among Bodrum's working people undoubtedly made him qualified to speak about the 'folk', with whom the Blue-ists attempted to define a unique Anatolian culture. The natural common sense and wisdom of the ordinary man and woman, they believed, had been handed down since the times of Homer, and it came from their intimate relationship with nature, with the seasons, the winds, the earth and the sea.

Cevat Şakir can also be seen mirrored in time across southern Europe, much of which was emerging from the dark of a pre-industrial age into the electric light of the 20th century. In Italy there was Carlo Levi, also in internal exile, who wrote about the poor cave dwellers of the malarial south in *Christ Stopped at*

Eboli. In Spain Gerald Brenan attracted the Bloomsbury Set to his peasant existence in the Alpujarras, written up in *South From Grenada*. The ordinary Greek was extolled, too, by Nikos Kazantzakis in the character of Zorba. All these writers, like the Fisherman, possessed a profound humanity, which was given its voice through the lives of the poor.

In Turkey, a movement of 'village literature' was exemplified in the work of Sebahattin Alí. Born in what is now Bulgaria, Alí taught German in Aydın and Konya and wrote short stories about life in Anatolia where he had been a teacher in the Village Institutes. Branded a subversive, he was several times imprisoned and denied a passport. In 1948 he was shot near the Bulgarian border while trying to escape. Two years later Mahmut Makal's *Bizim Köy* (*A Village in Anatolia*) recorded the grinding poverty of the communities, barefoot in summer corn-stubble and through winter snow, where women were beaten by their husbands if they had not made bread by dawn. It shocked the literary elite of Istanbul, many of whom were descended from families that came from the city or from the glamorous parts of the former empire, who had long ignored backward Anatolia. Now they began to realise that this was their country: it was all they had left.

Although not engaged in political activity, the Blue Anatolian Humanists were proselytisers, giving talks and making films to reinforce their beliefs, and influencing Turkey's liberal left. Cevat Şakir never missed an opportunity to drive home the importance and relevance of the ancient civilisations of the Aegean and Mediterranean in his weekly programme on Izmir Radio, broadcast in the late 1960s. He would point out over and again that the roots of Western civilisation came from Anatolia and the Aegean. Their paternity was not in doubt: Homer 'father of Western literature', Herodotus 'father of history', Thales 'father of philosophy', Hippocrates 'father of medicine', Leucippus, "father of atomism", Pythagoras, 'father of geometry', Aristacchus 'father of astronomy'…

"To enumerate all the fathers of civilisation who came from Anatolia would take a conference lasting several hours," he said in a broadcast. In 1971 the Minister of Culture and Tourism of Turkey honoured him with a State Cultural Award.

Sailing along the coasts of Caria and Lycia, close to nature among an abundance of ruins with so many echoes of the past, Blue Voyagers will begin to feel a sense of the Fisherman of Halicarnassus's Blue Anatolian Humanism and his believe that this is where Western civilisation began.

12. WOMEN, GODDESSES
& MOTHER SEA

Women were important to Cevat Şakir: his mother, his wives, his sisters, his daughters. His mother, Sare İsmet, was fourteen years old when she married his father. Şakir Pasha picked her out from among schoolgirls to whom he was presenting diplomas in Rethymnon, Crete. In his mid-thirties, he had been posted as regional commandant and aide-de-camp to his brother, who was acting military commander of the island.

Cevat was the first of seven siblings: three brothers and two sisters by Sare İsmet and an older step-brother from his father's first marriage to a Hungarian woman about whom little seems to be known, except that she died giving birth to Âsim. The children were all intelligent and artistic, and their father's encouragement helped them become one of the leading cultural families in Turkey. Aliye, the youngest, made her name as the first woman engraver in Turkey. Fahrelnisssa, who married Prince Zeid bin Huseyin, brother of King Faisal I, to become mother of Crown Prince Ra'ad, was also a considerable artist. She remembered being encouraged to paint at the age of four by her seventeen-year-old brother, Cevat.

"The sound of his brush came to my ears like a melody. He held my hand and started moving it on the paper. Since that day, neither that sound has vanished, nor the passion for painting." And she recalled him telling her: *"Well done, Nissa. I love the bold strokes*

of your pencil. For someone your age you have an amazing perspective. You are talented, my dear."

These anecdotes come from the catalogue of an exhibition of Fahrelnisssa Zeid's work at Istanbul Modern in 2006, fifteen years after her death. In 2012 a job lot of her paintings went under the hammer at Bonham's in London, including three sketch portraits of her brother, in one of which he looks particularly dapper in a wide collared coat and dandy hat. They fetched £1,875.

Cevat Şakir 's marriage to his cousin did not survive his exile. His third wife, Hatice, was a Cretan whose family had settled in Bodrum during the population exchange. They had three children, and by all accounts they were close. Ostracised by the family he had been born into, he put great store in the family he created. He was out on a three-day expedition with sponge divers when a telegram from Istanbul arrived to say that his mother was seriously ill. He reached the city hospital in time for a brief reconciliation and she died in his arms. It had been twenty-four years since they had seen each other.

İsmet, his oldest daughter by Hatice, was involved in the setting up of the Cevat Şakir exhibition in Bodrum Maritime Museum in 2012, providing much of the memorabilia, from books to baby clothes. "The museum should have been created years ago," she said at the opening ceremony, adding, "I am so affected by the objects here, I could cry." Many of the items had come from the family house the Fisherman had bought in Gümbet, on the west side of Bodrum, which after his death and until the museum was established had been open to the public.

Some see the word Anadolu in Turkish as meaning "full of mothers". Cevat Şakir believed that Anatolia had a matriarchal society, and his experience in Bodrum may have reinforced this view. Fatma Mansur, who lived here through the winter of 1967–68 researching her book *Bodrum: a Town in the Aegean*, noticed that when a man and wife travelled from the town, it was the woman who sat on the donkey and not the man, as happened in other parts of the country.

The Fisherman also looked to Anatolia's heroines and goddesses from the earliest times to bolster his case. Here in Anadolu, the motherland, not the fatherland, was the very dawn of civilisation. He was delighted when Çatalhöyük, the largest known Neolithic site at the time, dating from 7500BC, was discovered in 1958. Wall paintings and statuary showed strong evidence of a supreme Mother Goddess.

From the Hittites, whose chief deity was the Sun Goddess Arinitte, he traces a direct line from their Mother Goddess Hepa to the Olympian Hebe and the Biblical Eve.

In Classical times, Cybele, the Earth-Mother Goddess sacred to Mount Ida (Kazdağı) near Troy, was the most important deity of Anatolia. And it was from the Black Sea coast of northeast Anatolia that the Amazon warriors came. Cevat Şakir suggests that they were in fact the educated priestesses of the Hittites, who worshipped the Mother Goddess. Their accomplishments included the harnessing of horses for chariots and the deployment of cavalry long before the Greeks. Reaching the Aegean, they defeated the Trojans, subdued many islands such as Lesbos, Lemnos and Samos, and founded the cities of Smyrna, Kyme, Priene and Ephesus, which were named after their leaders. Amazons were associated with the introduction of the cult of the Great Anatolian Mother Goddess, Artemis of Ephesus, and it is perhaps no surprise that the city much later became the centre of the Christian Marian cult.

When Cevat Şakir was acting as a tourist guide to Ephesus, the House of the Virgin Mary was on his itinerary, and he witnessed Pope Paul VI's visit to the shrine in 1967. This is the house where the most venerated woman in Christianity apparently lived after the crucifixion, when she is said to have travelled to the Roman capital in Asia Minor with the apostle John.

The site had been identified in visions by a bedridden German nun, the Blessed Anne Catherine Emerich, and located by a French priest, Abbé Julien Gouyet, in 1881. Today the small building on a mountainside overlooking the ancient city is a place of pilgrimage. As the only woman mentioned in the Koran, where her name crops up thirty times, the Virgin Mary is venerated by Muslims as Miryam Ana, Mother Mary, and they join Christians gathering here on August 15, the day of her Assumption.

Mary's House, a book about its discovery published in 2000, was written by the late American author Donald Carroll, who lived for a short time on the Bodrum peninsula and was a friend of Mehmet Bas, often called 'Bodrum's last sponge diver' Mehmet is also a poet, and as a tribute to his fellow writer, he commissioned a marble plaque dedicated to Carroll, which he erected on the seabed as a permanent memorial to his friend.

The pantheon of Anatolian divinities is underpinned by an earthly gallery of heroic Carian women, whose achievements Cevat Şakir could admire and write about.

The earliest was Artemisia I of Halicarnassus, the first known female naval commander, one of four to join Xerxes in the second Persian invasion of Greece in 480BC. She led a fleet of five ships from Halicarnassus and the neighbouring islands into battle at Salamis. Though the Greeks were victorious, Artemisia broke through the Greek lines without loss. According to Herodotus, Xerxes afterwards said: "Today men fought like women and women like men." The Athenians, outraged that a woman should defy them, put a 10,000 drachma price on her head.

Artemisia II is in the history books for conquering the island of Rhodes. On the death of her brother-husband Mausolos in 353BC, the people of Rhodes, sensing weakness, had attacked Halicarnassus. Forewarned, Artemisia hid the Carian ships in a creek behind the palace on which the castle now stands, and after the enemy had stepped ashore, she pounced, surrounding their ships and towing them out to sea, leaving those on land to be butchered. The Rhodian ships were then manned with Carians who towed their own fleet towards Rhodes. The sight of the Carian vessels being brought triumphantly home made the people of Rhodes believe they had been victorious. Caught unguarded, the city was overcome by the queen and her forces.

The third of the triumvirate of queens was Orantabatis, who held out heroically against Alexander the Great as he came marching through, driving down the coast on his way to India to build the largest empire the Classical world had ever known. It took the Macedonian king three months to breach the city walls, and the Carians held out in the fortifications on Zephyros and Salmakis at either side of the harbour for a further year. Finally, inevitably, they succumbed and the city was burned, though the citizens were spared.

Ada I, King Mausolos's sister and the last of the Hecatomnid dynasty he had created, replaced Queen Orantabatis. She formally adopted Alexander the Great as her son, so the territory would pass to him and his heirs on her death, which it did. However, the terrible destruction he had wrought meant the end of Halicarnassus as a town or port of any significance.

Queen Ada I came back to life in 1989 when a sarcophagus belonging to a Carian noble woman was found during building work on the site of what was the town's ancient necropolis. Gold and jewellery in the chamber included a ring with a portrait of its wearer, a likeness that matched the head that was rebuilt from the skull by scientists at Manchester University. The skeleton was dated to the time of Queen Ada and the woman had died at the right age, around forty-four. The reconstructed head and robed figure, which can be seen in a room dedicated to her in Bodrum Castle Museum, looks much like a bust of Ada found at Priene and now in the British Museum.

Whether these queens were pioneers for their sex, or whether they were the result of a more equitable society is impossible to say, but as Cevat Şakir pointed out, in antiquity the women of Anatolia were not treated like slaves, unlike Hellenic Greece where they were hidden away, stepping out only when veiled and accompanied by servants. Anatolian society was more inclusive.

It is therefore perhaps unsurprising that the first revelations of women's bodies in Classical sculpture come from Anatolia. These sensual, life-size sea nymphs from around 385BC are now in the Lycian Room of the British Museum, where the Fisherman would have seen them when he was a student in England. The figures were taken from the Nereid, the tomb of Arbina, ruler of Xanthos in Lycia. Riding the waves, the nymphs' clothes have become transparent, clinging to their bodies, revealing the contours of the full shape of their breasts and the deep well of their bellies. This was the final stage in the development of sculptures from the geometric figures of Egypt, and they are looked on as milestones in Western art.

It was Praxiteles, the best-known Athenian sculptor, who took away the last shreds of clothing to create the first fully nude female sculpture, which was made especially for an

Anatolian public. The statue of the goddess of Aphrodite is said to have been modelled by Phryne, a famously beautiful courtesan, and it showed her preparing to bathe, with her clothes in her left hand while her right hand covered her modesty. According to Pliny, this came about because two statues had been ordered for a temple on the island of Kos. One was naked, one clothed, and the people of Kos, rather shocked, settled for the clothed version. But the residents of neighbouring Knidos, opposite Bodrum across the gulf, gladly took the rejected woman and installed her in their temple overlooking the sea, where passing sailors could seek her blessing. Curiously, in this ancient world of bare-breasted Amazons and men who played and fought naked, the statue of an unclothed woman aroused enormous appreciation and it became something of a tourist attraction.

The last recorded sighting of Aphrodite of Knidos comes from the fifth century when she was apparently taken by the Christian Emperor Theodosias to his palace in Constantinople where she fell victim to the conflagrations of the Nike revolt of AD532. Though much copied, particularly as the Roman Venus, the protectress of seafarers had long gone by the time Cevat Şakir saw the ancient settlement and felt compelled to compose an essay on the statue, likening it to *"a moon shining over the city".* Feeling the life force of the peerless goddess of love, he declared: *"Life is such that the mutually created should love one another. Because if they do something other than love one other, they will be the executioners of one another."*

Standing on this extreme southwest tip of Anatolia, where the waters of the Aegean and Mediterranean mingle, looking across the bay to the islands from Kos to Rhodes, he could contemplate the many mysteries of the sea from its endless blue to the microscopic plasma that sustained its teaming inhabitants. In every cubic metre, he pointed out, lay 40 million small creatures that would whiten the waters on spring and summer nights, producing what he called 'sea milk'. It was always the land, with its Earth-Mother Goddess in the mountains, that was associated with fertility and productivity.

"*However, the real symbol of motherhood is the sea*," he wrote. "*The sea is the giant breast that suckles all living things*."

13. ECOLOGY

"This deep blue sky of southern Anatolia, its violet sea, light and land, has nourished various trees, fruits, flowers, human being and civilisations. These stories too are the product of these heavenly hands, mountains, grass, coasts, wild rocks, ruins and open seas. I dedicate all the stories to them."

These words are from the introduction to a collection of essays by the Fisherman of Halicarnassus titled *A Flower Left to the Aegean Sea*. Flowers and plants were as important to Cevat Şakir as the fish in the sea, and he has been described as 'Turkey's first ecologist' Every October 13, the anniversary of his death, a tree is planted in Bodrum in his memory. He is remembered, too, on the palm trees that lead up to the town hall at the harbour end of the street that bears his name. Each one has a small metal plaque nailed to it with the title of one of Halikarnas Balıkçısı's books. This was the man, after all, who did so much to make the town not just a greener, but a much more colourful place.

The bougainvillea that so lights up the white walls in gorgeous shades of pink is his doing – he introduced the shrub to the town. He was the first to plant grapefruit here, too, and eucalyptus trees: he planted the one now outside Bodrum Maritime Museum in 1938, and it now bears a plaque commemorating the first Cevat Şakir festival organised by Bodrum municipality in 2003. But most of all he is remembered for importing and planting the palms that give the harbour an exotic air.

From the outset of his exile, Cevat Şakir cast his artistic eye over Bodrum and thought of the colourful plants that might add to its charm. The locals were good plantsmen, but in their practical world the earth was for providing sustenance, and most of their gardens were filled with fruit trees and vegetable plants, as many still are today.

The Fisherman served only eighteen months of his three-year sentence in the town, after which he was sent back to Constantinople to complete the term. In the city, as he dreamed of returning to Bodrum, he read all he could about agriculture and horticulture, and after his release he went straight back to the same small white seaside house that he had first occupied, armed with a large selection of seeds and plants. Unrestricted now in his movements, he continued to order books, plants and seeds from around the world, filling his pockets with collected seeds and scattering them liberally. He dug up seedlings, took cuttings, and imported soil and fertiliser by boat and donkey. Horticultural jottings and tips that he kept in a notebook were passed around town.

One flower took his fancy while he was translating *Carmen*. In Prosper Mérimée's novel, the Andalusian cigar girls wore yellow cassia flowers in their hair, so he ordered some seeds from Paris and was delighted some years later to see girls in Bodrum wearing them. He also introduced the Bella Sombra from South America. This huge evergreen tree produces enormous branches like the fingers of an upturned hand, creating a wide canopy to provide a perfect shady spot on a hot summer's day.

The lack of colourful flowers Cevat Şakir initially found in the town was more than made up for by nature in the surrounding countryside. Turkey has a spectacular range of wild flowers, and among the hills and valleys of Caria and the Taurus mountains of Lycia, there is great diversity. The 800-km Carian Trail and the 500-km Lycian Way are two recently introduced long-distance footpaths that provide a way of exploring the area. Here are wild gladioli, black fritillaries, yellow asphodel, snowdrops, and the hyacinths and orchids whose edible bulbs are used in ice-creams and *salep*, the hot winter drink. There are plants used by weavers to dye kilim rugs, bright orange stripped barks of frankincense trees and forests of oriental sweetgum. The land around the ancient sites of Anatolia is particularly rich in wild plants, which have flourished undisturbed by fork or plough for 2,000 years.

"Take a blind man to Lycia," wrote the Fisherman, *"and he will immediately know from the smell of the air exactly where he is. The acrid perfume of lavender, the pungent fragrance of wild mint and thyme, will tell him."*

One of the friends that he took on his Blue Voyages was an Izmir pharmacist called Tekin. His son Erdoğan went along, too, and the voyages sparked a life-long interest in nature. In 2007, after twenty-five years spent photographing the wildflowers of Turkey as a hobby, Erdoğan Tekin's two-volume bilingual (Turkish-English) *The Most Beautiful Wild Flowers of Turkey* was published with more than 1,500 photographs. It was an instant success and it remains the most comprehensive field guide to the country's flora.

The countryside also provided sustenance for Blue Voyagers, who could forage for fruit and berries as well as for herbs to add to the fish that they fried. At the end of his sentence in Constantinople, Cevat Şakir had purchased what fishing equipment he could to take back to Bodrum where had would reel in groupers, bluefish, gilt-head bream, mullet, turbot. He studied the behaviour of sealife, too, and wrote about it in an essay titled 'The Craftsmanship of the Mediterranean Fish.'

The sea no longer turns white with the teaming shoals of fish that he described, but Blue Voyage charters today often pick up fresh catches from villages to cook for their passengers, and there's usually a line on board with something from the galley that can be used as bait. The range of species can be seen in the small stalls that fishermen set up on Bodrum's harbourside, but there is a better display in the market half way up Cevat Şakir Caddesi. Here traditional *meyhane* eating houses sit alongside fishmongers, so diners can choose their fish for the restaurants to cook, for just a few lira, while eating a variety of *mezes*.

Some bream and bass come from fish farms in the area. But these are controversial, as their pellet feed contaminates the water, making it cloudy. Everyone is acutely aware of conservation and the need to protect endangered species. There is a moratorium on large fishing boats operating during the summer, trawlers are not allowed closer than 1.5 nautical miles from the shore. Seiners, which trap fish in great drawstring nets, are banned in water less than eighteen metres deep. Quotas are applied to bluefin tuna and other species whose stocks are diminishing. All marine mammals are protected by law, including whales and dolphins, of which there are several species.

The many underwater caves around Gökova and the Bodrum peninsula provide breeding grounds for the protected Mediterranean monk seals, though overfishing has depleted foodstocks, which has reduced their numbers. Also protected are the breeding grounds of the sandbar shark in Boncuk Bay opposite Sedir island on the southeast side of the Gulf of Gökova. There are said to be otters in the wetlands around

Akyaka at the head of the Gulf where there are white-breasted kingfishers and many other bird species. But urbanisation has taken a toll. North of Bodrum, golf links and other developments have reduced the flamingo population of Lake Tuzla and caused major wildlife depletion.

The other significant species facing danger is the loggerhead turtle, which lays its eggs on İztuzu beach near Dalyan. Protection for the beach was won only in 1988 after a major battle with developers. There are many protected park areas around Bodrum. The entire Gökova Gulf is a marine reserve and a marine park was established in 2009 in the Kaş-Kekova area of the Lycian coast, with plans to extend it further.

Such conservation concerns did not exist in Cevat Şakir's time, though the first signs of trouble were already evident in the decline of sponge stocks. In his day, nature was pristine and abundant, fertilising his creativity. Only 5,000 people lived in the town then. Today, that entire population could fill the Halikarnas disco, the most famous in Turkey, built on the seashore east of the castle half a dozen years after the Fisherman's death, with laser lights that can be seen thirty kilometres away. It's a modern Wonder of the Entertainment World, and probably far better known than old Mausolos's tomb. In summer Bodrum's resident 50,000 population expands to more than half a million, and the pressure this puts on the environment creates ecological problems that were hard to imagine half a century ago.

Sabahattin Eyüboğlu had told Azra Erhat: "One day will come when we don't want to be in Bodrum, even if it will be for going on a Blue Voyage."

But that was not how Cevat Şakir felt. He was, she wrote, fully aware that the town would be developed but he wanted as many people as possible to come to share his experiences of

117

Blue Voyages and to be seduced by its blue seas, its landscapes and ancient monuments. His vision went beyond the small village he had first known to a new Halicarnassus, a major city in his Sixth Continent, where more and more people would come to see this captivating corner of Turkey.

He didn't even complain when his Bella Ombra trees were uprooted to make way for a new main road.

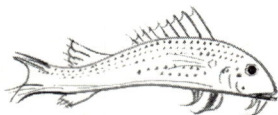

14. ISLANDS OF DREAMS

A kind of magic prevails among the lands of the Blue Voyages, and it is no surprise that legends and fanciful tales are attached to them. The Fisherman of Halicarnassus described the islands floating like clouds, ready to be picked up and used as pillows. He loved to hear his 'Hello's echo in their bays, and he thought the islands so pristine and innocent that to relieve himself on them felt as embarrassing as dirtying the face of a child.

In *The Journeying Moon*, Ernle Bradford wrote: "*Every island is a revelation. You leave one behind and the sea enfolds you, deep as a dream. The next island is a fresh awakening. It swims up out of the Aegean, pearled with cloud in the early morning, or shining like a hard gem at noon, or pulling the night over it, like an old cloak and twinkling with lights along its sea-worn quay.*"

Watching these ancient lands pass by on a Blue Voyage can arouse many fanciful thoughts, and it is easy to understand why they brought forth the gods and legends of antiquity. Inventing stories of fabulous or miraculous incidents – the Cove of the Merciful Mermaid, the Bay of the Bemused Bear, The Island of the Self-Sacrificing Goats – are the stuff of genial sailing companionship, just as ghost stories rise up with the flames of winter fires.

The silence of the seas might be broken by the flip of a tail disturbing the water's surface, the rustle of a foraging goat, the honk of a seal or the grunt of a bear. Brown bears inhabited the area in the Fisherman's day, before developments drove them away. They were annoyed if they were disturbed and would stand on the shore and throw stones with alarming accuracy at boats that came near.

The stories that the Fisherman of Halicarnassus made up included the autobiography of a donkey who complained that he and his ancestors had been carrying the village economy on their backs for 500 years, and the story of Crazy David whose smiling ways attracted Laughing Island and made its shores and plants breezily excited every time he came near. According to his daughter, İsmet, the idea for a story first entered the author's imagination as a mental image, which he would swiftly draw. He would then screw up the paper and throw it into a bin before settling down to write. İsmet recalls rummaging in his bins to rescue the drawings. His style was often a quick and easy caricature, and his uncomplicated drawings, particularly of items from antiquity, were rendered in firm lines or with hatches and crosshatches.

The Greek name for the Aegean was *Archepelagos* (Αρχι–principal, πέλαγο–sea). Its myriad islands are the result of tectonic plates colliding after the last Ice Age, and the Aegean remains one of the most seismically exciting parts of the world. It is truly the land of Poseidon, Lord of the Earthquakes, and minor tremors occur every day. Temples, towns and whole civilisations have been felled by his blows. From the nearby islands of Kos, Gyali and Nisyros, the South Aegean Volcanic Arc stretches across the sea to Santorini and Aegina, close to Athens.

An earthquake in 1933 demolished much of the town of Kos – only to reveal the ancient city beneath, which the occupying Italians were then able to excavate. Cevat Şakir would have felt the tremors, which brought down the minaret of Bodrum's New Mosque. Nisyros is another popular Blue

Voyage excursion, and guides here lead visitors into an active volcano's steaming caldera floor.

The Fisherman saw Bodrum Peninsula as the place where these islands had been born. He described the ones nearby as circles of fairies surrounding the peninsula, while further out the Cyclades and Sporades made a larger circle, like the scattering of seeds by some giant's sweeping hand. The islands in the Gulf of Gökova have their own descriptive names: Cattle (Sığır), Forked (Çatal), Pious (Sali), Pointed (Sivri), Tile-like (Keremit), Sickle (Orak) Thicket (Kisle-Bükü) and one of the Fisherman's favourites, just opposite Bodrum, Black Island (Kara Ada), which has hot springs and mud baths.

Myths and legends take root and are nurtured here. Among the sirens is Cleopatra, whose name crops up in bays and coves. Mark Antony, taking the eastern half of the Roman Empire, had arrived in triumph in Ephesus, presenting himself as Bacchus, the Greek Dionysius, god of wine and pleasure. To win his support, the Egyptian queen turned up in Tarsus dressed as Venus, the Greek Aphrodite. Reported Pliny: *"The word went all through the multitude that Venus was come to feast with Bacchus for the common good of Asia."* Cleopatra reclined beneath a golden canopy on a barge rowed with silver oars, surrounded by neirids and serenaded by music in a cloud of perfume. She gave herself to him and he gave her the Mediterranean coast of Anatolia, so the story goes. From this moment her name drifted westward along the coast, reaching the Gulf of Gökova on Sedir (Cedar) Island where the fine sand on Cleopatra's Beach was reputedly imported from Egypt by Mark Antony. En route is Cleopatra's Bay (Manastır Bay), near Göcek, where she supposedly bathed in the mineral-rich hot spring. A more recent Egyptian ruler, Prince Regent Muhammad Abdul Moneim, who had married the last Sultan's granddaughter, owned Pig Island (Domuz Adasi) where he liked to tell visitors about the island's wild pigs that swam in the sea.

Long before the Fisherman dreamed up a talking donkey, many animals were ascribed human powers. For the ancients, dolphins were quite capable of rescuing people at sea and raising lost children. Coins found at Iassos, just north of Bodrum, show a boy riding a dolphin, which relates to a tale from Pliny, who says the dolphin used to pick up the boy on the shore here when he was bathing to take him joy-riding, before returning him safely at the end of the day. The story attracted Alexander the Great when he was here, and he summoned the boy to Babylon to make him a priest of Poseidon, god of the sea, who in mythology was served by dolphins. Further back in time, Homer's *Hymn to Apollo* relates how the son of Zeus disguised himself as a dolphin to hijack a ship to reach Delphi (*delphis* is Greek for dolphin) where the sailors erected his principal temple. In Turkish folk tales dolphins take on the role of a dashing seaborne cavalry that protects the shore.

Dolphins are the subject of the Fisherman's 'Seals and Dolphins', in which he describes how one winter he befriended a seal on Kara Ada, where they would sit together and watch the sea. Seals were often referred to as "rascals" and were the subjects of many local tales. One describes gendarmes arresting a seal, thinking he was a moustachioed Peeping Tom spying on women bathers. Cevat Şakir wrote down a story told by an old fisherman called Selim, who claimed he had spent the night on a beach where seals had come ashore. There in the moonlight they had removed their coats to lie down to sleep, revealing humans beneath. The female who lay down next to him was a blue-eyed redhead with legs "like a pair of gushing springs". He fell in love with her, hid her coat and won her affections, taking him back to his home, where she bore him two children, until she discovered her coat that he had hidden. Putting it on, she dashed back into the sea. After that she would return twice a night to kiss her children.

The Fisherman of Halicarnassus never had to go far to find his stories. Sometimes it was enough just to daydream.

15. TOMBSTONES

The old cemetery up behind yacht club where Mustafa Pasha of Kızılhisar and his son Cafer Pasha are entombed is a place to wander away from the crowds. Here gravestones evoke the past lives of the better-off who once lived in the town. Inscriptions are mostly in the Arabic script of Ottoman Turkey, though a few use Latin letters, showing it was still in use after 1928 when the new alphabet was introduced. The much larger modern cemetery is up by the Myndos Gate, the western entry to Mausolos's city. Here the sea captains and common folk of the town are buried in blazing white marble graves, their headstones etched with epitaphs.

The Fisherman of Halicarnassus enjoyed spending time in graveyards where he collected some of the more flamboyant sayings. One day in Izmir his youngest sister Aliye introduced him to John Freely, the American writer and historian who edited *Golden Horn*, an annual literary magazine published in Istanbul during the 1960s. Following a conversation about how the lives of the people of the Aegean coast affected their spirit and philosophy, Freely asked the Fisherman if he would contribute a piece on the subject for his magazine. In the subsequent article titled 'Laughing Tombstones' the Fisherman cited some of his favourite epitaphs, which Freely quotes in his 1988 book, *The Western Shores of Turkey*:

"A pity to good-hearted Ismail Efendi, whose death caused great sadness among his friends. Having caught the illness of love at the

age of seventy he took the bit between his teeth and dashed full gallop to paradise."

"*Stopping his ears with his fingers, Judge Mehmet hied off from this beautiful world, leaving his wife's cackling and his mother-in-law's gabbling."*

On a wayside tomb: "*Oh passerby, spare me your prayers, but please don't steal my tombstone!"*

"*I could have died as well without a doctor as with the quack that friends had set upon me."*

"*I have swerved away from you for a long time. But in soil, air, cloud, rain, plant, flower, butterfly or bird, I am always with you."*

On a tombstone with the relief of three trees: an almond, a cypress, and a peach-tree – a peach being the Turkish metaphor for a breast: "*I've planted these trees so that people might know my fate. I loved an almond-eyed, cypress-tall maiden, and bade farewell to this beautiful world without savouring her peaches."*

Cevat Şakir died of bone cancer in Izmir on October 13, 1973. His last words were reported to be: "*Oh this is such a pain. Nature has locked my hand at a crucial moment... I guess I am leaving. I will just say hello to the world and leave. I can smell flowers. Open the windows. I want to see the sun one last time. I want to see this unique land one last time. Hello children, hello world. Hello."*

His coffin was taken to Bodrum where the whole town turned out to pay their respects. Among the mourners were his daughter İsmet and her American husband John Noonon, who described the scene to a letter to Alfred Friendly, a former editor of the *Washington Post*, as "*the most incredible experience of my life…As we drive down Cevat Şakir Caddesi virtually everybody turned out to line the streets – a wholesale communal showing of life – schoolchildren spaced out with flowers, hundreds upon hundreds of peasants and fishermen…A truly magnificent sight for a truly magnificent human being."*

Put aboard a fishing boat, the coffin was taken out of the harbour and round to Gümbet where his home had been. "The Fisherman of Halicarnassus was able to say farewell to his beloved Kara Ada island and Salmakis," İsmet recalls. "The boat carried the coffin all around the bay, and then rounded the castle where it was brought ashore. There was a call in the harbour: 'Only the fishermen should come forth'. And my father's coffin was entrusted to them."

He was buried on a hill behind Gümbet opposite the simple house he had loved, looking over blue sea and the town that had become forever associated with his name. In time his house opened as a museum where people could see where and how he lived. Then, in 2012, some of its contents were transferred to an exhibition space in the new Bodrum Maritime Museum off Cevat Şakir Caddesi in the centre of town. There are hopes that the house will one day open again, perhaps as a café, where a little of his simple life and times can be savoured.

The Blue Anatolian Humanist had provided his own epitaph when he wrote: "*The heavenly bliss of life in Bodrum is better than any eternal bliss that may await us.*"

TIME LINE

Prehistory

9000BC Göbekli Tepe, southeast Anatolia, the oldest known human-made religious structure.

7000BC Çatalhöyük, southern Anatolia, largest known neolithic settlement.

3000BC emigrations from Anatolia to Crete and Greece

16th–14thC BC First known mention of Carians, in Hittite texts. Anatolian Hittites contol Asia Minor, with a capital in Hattusa. Amazons from around the River Thermodon (Terme) in northern Anatolia move west, reaching the Aegean, their queens founding Ephesus and Smyrna (Izmir).

1400BC Uluburun shipwreck off Cape Gelidonya, now in Bodrum Castle Museum.

c.1190BC Siege of Troy. Carians allied to Trojans.

Greeks and Carians

c.800BC Homer's *Iliad* and *Odyssey*

c.700BC Dorians arrive from Peleponnese, settling on Bodrum's island of Zephyros and to the south. Ionian settlers follow, settling in Bodrum and on the coast to the north.

c.480BC Herodotus born in Halicarnassus

446BC Caria joins Attika-Delian Sea League, bringing Athenian culture and colonialism.

412BC Carian uprising against Greeks.

377–353BC King Mausolos moves Carian capital from Mylasa (Milas) to Halicarnassus.

334BC Halicarnassus conquered by Alexander the Great, ending its importance as a sea port.

192BC Anatolia becomes the Roman province of Asia. Its capital city, Ephesus, is the largest in the empire outside Rome.

Foundation of Constantinople

AD330 Constantinople (Istanbul) founded by Constantine, the first Roman Emperor to convert to Christianity.

395 Roman Empire divided between East and West. Caria comes under the see of the Archbishopric of Aphrodisias.

529 Antiquity ends with the closure of the philosophical schools.

632 Death of the Prophet Muhammad.

638 Jerusalem taken by Muslim armies.

7th–8thC The Roman Empire of the East is transformed into the medieval state of Byzantium.

First Turkish arrivals

1060 Seljuk Turks (Sunni Muslims and ancestors of the modern Turks) arrive from central Asia, conquering central and southern Anatolia, including Halicarnassus (1071). The resulting Sultinate of Rum, with capitals in Iznik (Nicaea) and Konya (Iconium) is eventually divided into beyliks (hence bey, meaning chief). Bodrum comes under the beylik of Menteşe (1260–1425), with its capital at Milas.

1099 Jerusalem taken by Crusaders.

1187 Saladin, Sultan of Egypt, retakes Jerusalem.

1204 Crusaders sack Christian Constantinople.

1243 Seljuks defeated by Mongols and become their vassals.

1299 Osman Bey, from the Selkjuk beylik of Osmanoğlu, establishes a small Anatolian kingdom with the first capital in Bursa, to become founder of the 623-year dynastic rulers of the Ottoman Empire.

1309 Knights of St John fall back from Cyprus to Rhodes and begin fortifying islands in the Dodecanese, as well as Izmir.

1402 Timur's Mongols invade Anatolia, taking Ankara and destroying the fortress of the Knights of St John in Izmir.

1406 Mehmet I Çelebi restores Ottoman Empire and grants Knights of St John permission to build St Peter's Castle (Peterion) in Bodrum.

1424 Beylik of Menteşe is absorbed into Ottoman Empire.

Fall of Constantinople

1453 Fall of Constantinople to Mehmet the Conqueror, beginning Ottoman rule, in which the Dodecanese form the Vilayet of the Islands.

1522 Süleyman the Magnificent takes Rhodes, and the Knights of St John lose all Turkish strongholds, including Bodrum.

1538 Ottoman fleet under Barbarossa defeats combined Christian forces at Preveza.

1770 Ottoman shipyard built in Bodrum

1832 Greece achieves independence.

1856 Charles Newton excavates the Mausoleum of Halicarnassus

1890 Cevat Şakir Kabaağaçlı born.

Turkish Independence

1908 Young Turk Revolution. North African territories lost to the Italians.

1912–13 First Balkan Wars: Ottomans lose all European territory, including Salonica and Crete, except for a part of Thrace. A million refugees flood into Turkey.

1914 Cevat Şakir shoots his father and is sentenced to seven years in prison.

1914–18 Ottomans allied to Germany in the First World War.

1918–23 British, French and Italians occupy Istanbul.

1919–22 Turkish War of Independence. Greek forces land at Izmir (**1919**) and begin invasion. Italians land at Antalya, and move inland and along coast to Bodrum.

1922 Ottoman Sultinate abolished.

1923 Turkish Republic declared with Mustafa Kemal (Atatürk) first president. Treaty of Lausanne results in Greek-Turkish population exchange and defines Tukey's borders.

The Fisherman's era

1925 Cevat Şakir arrives in Bodrum.

1938 Death of Atatürk.

1939–45 Second World War. Turkey remains neutral until near the end.

1947 Italians cede Dodecanese to Greece. Cevat Şakir and his family move to Izmir.

1953 4th-century bust of Demeter found by *gangava* diver.

1961 Bodrum Museum created in Bodrum castle.

1973 Cevat Şakir dies in Izmir. Institute of Nautical Archaeology established in Bodrum.

1989 First Bodrum Cup, annual regatta for traditional boats.

2012 Bodrum Maritime Museum opens.

2013 Events in Bodrum commemorate **40**th anniversary of Cevat Şakir's death.

MORE BOOKS FOR THE BUNK-SIDE

Akşit, İlhan *Lycia: The Land of Light*, Akşit Kültür ve Turızm Yayincilik, Istanbul, **2006**

Bass, George *Archaeologist Beneath the Sea: Ancient Ships in Bodrum*, Boyut, Turkey, **2013**

Beaufort, Francis *Karamania, or a Brief Description of the South Coast of Asia-Minor and of the Remains of Antiquity. With plans, views, &c. collected during a survey of that coast, under the orders of the Lords commissioners of the Admiralty, in the years 1811-1812*

Bean, George Ewart *Aegean Turkey, Turkey Beyond the Maeander, Turkey's Southern Shore, Lycian Turkey*, all John Murray, London

Bradford, Ernle *The Sultan's Admiral: The Life of Barbarossa*, London, **1968**; *Ulysses Unbound*; *The Great Siege: Malta 1565*; *The Shield and the Sword*

Bruce Clark *Twice a Stranger: How Mass Expulsion Forged Modern Greee and Turkey*, Granta Books, London, **2006**

Devrim, Shirin *A Turkish Tapestry: The Shakirs of Istanbul*, Quartet Books, London, **1994**

Freely, John *The Western Shores of Turkey*, John Murray, London **1988**; *The Aegean Coast of Turkey*, Redhouse Press, Istanbul, **1996**

Herodotus *The Histories*

Homer *Odyssey*, *Iliad*

Kinross, Lord, *Europa Minor*, John Murray, London, **1956**

Kücükeren, C. Canan *Karia, an Anatolian Civilisation in the Aegean*, Istanbul

Mansur, Fatma *Bodrum, a Town in the Aegean*, E.J. Brill, Leiden, **1972**

Mango, Andrew *Atatürk, the Biography of the Founder of Modern Turkey*, **1997**; *The Turks Today*, **2004**, both John Murray, London

Rogerson, Barnaby *The Last Crusaders: The Battle for Gold, God and Dominion*, Little, Brown, London, **2009**

Stark, Freya *Ionia: A Quest*, **1954**; *The Lycean Shore*, **1956**, both John Murray, London

Thonemann, Peter *The Maeander Valley: A Historical Geography from Antiquity to Byzantium*, Cambridge University Press, **2012**

Throckmorton, Peter *The Lost Ships*, Jonathan Cape, London **1965**

Books by Halikarnas Balıkçısı, the Fisherman of Halicarnassus

Novels *Aganta, Burina, Burinata* (1945), *Ötelerin Çocuğu* (1956), *Uluç Reis* (1962), *Turgut Reis* (1966), *Deniz Gurbetçileri* (1969)

Short stories *Ege Kıyılarından* (1939), *Merhaba Akdeniz* (1947), *Ege'nin Dibi* (1952), *Yaşasın Deniz* (1954), *Gülen Ada* (1957), *Ege'den* (1972), *Gençlik Denizlerinde* (1973), *Parmak Damgası* (1986), *Dalgıçlar* (1991), *Gündüzünü Kaybeden Kuş*

Essays *Anadolu Efsaneleri* (1954), *Anadolu Tanrıları* (1955), *Mavi Sürgün* (**autobiography**, 1961), *Anadolu'nun Sesi* (**analysis**, 1971), *Hey Koca Yurt* (1972), *Merhaba Anadolu* (1980), *Düşün Yazıları* (1981), *Altıncı Kıta Akdeniz* (1982), *Sonsuzluk Sessiz Büyür* (1983), *Çiçeklerin Düğünü* (1991), *Arşipel* (1993)

In English
Asia Minor, Interpreter-Guides and Tourism Association, Izmir, 1971
The Sixth Continent, Directorate General of Cultural Affairs of the Ministry of Foreign Affairs, Ankara, 1991
An Anthology of Modern Turkish Short Stories ('The Aegean Floor' and 'The Karabulut Family'), Biblioteca Islamica, Minneapolis, 1978
Contemporary Turkish Literature ('The Resurrection of the Unknown Soldier'), Fairleigh Dickinson University Press, London, 1982

INDEX

136